The Strategic Grant-Seeker

A Guide to Conceptualizing
Fundable Research
in the Brain and Behavioral
Sciences

The Strategic Grant-Seeker

A Guide to Conceptualizing Fundable Research in the Brain and Behavioral Sciences

Judy Illes, PhD

LAWRENCE ERLBAUM AND ASSOCIATES, PUBLISHERS

1999   Mahwah, New Jersey   London

Lawrence Erlbaum Associates, Inc., Publishers
10 Industrial Avenue
Mahwah, New Jersey 07430-2262

Cover design by Kathryn Houghtaling Lacey

Library of Congress Cataloging-in-Publication Data

The strategic grant-seeker : a guide to conceptualizing
fundable research in the brain and behavioral sciences / Judy
Illes.
    p. cm.
    Includes bibliographical references and index.
    ISBN 0-8058-2979-2 (alk. paper) 0-8058-2980-6
(pbk. : alk. paper)
    1. Neurosciences—Research grants. 2. Proposal writ-
ing for grants. I. Title.
RC377.I34 1999
612.8'079—dc21   98-31050
                                                   CIP

Books published by Lawrence Erlbaum Associates are
printed on acid-free paper, and their bindings are chosen for
strength and durability

Printed in the United States of America
10 9 8 7 6 5 4 3 2 1

The goal of competing is the perfect execution of a strategy
—KoDenKan Institute
for the martial arts

Contents

Preface

Successfully competing for research dollars requires strategy and skilled execution. The strategy resides in knowledge of the vast network of funding opportunities and in thoughtful planning to find a good match between a research idea and a prospective sponsor's priorities and interests. The execution resides in the ability to formulate a scientific plan that maximizes the match, in the proficiency to translate the plan into a written document, and in the ability to maintain a partnership with a sponsor. *The Strategic Grant-Seeker* is designed to serve as a resource for researchers and research-entrepreneurs in the brain and behavioral science disciplines who seek to build a complete toolbox of these strategies for funding success.

Chapter 1 focuses on the relationships among researchers, sponsors, and the funding environment. The chapter discusses the development of funding plans and means of accessing information and cultivating opportunities, sponsor funding power, payline, and award rates. Chapters 2 through 5 focus on four of the most common types of research for which funding is sought: research projects, multicomponent programs, career and training, and small business innovation. The emphasis in these chapters is on the conceptualization of a research idea, on the match between a concept and the requirements of a sponsor, and on critically evaluating concepts for competitiveness. Detailed decision pathways form the core of these chapters and fundamentally distinguish this book from others dedicated to grant writing only. Chapters 6 through 8 provide strategies for translating ideas into written proposals, preparing administrative sections, and communicating with sponsors. The final chapters, 9, 10, and 11, are dedicated to the outcomes of the proposal process: reviews, rebuttals and resubmissions, progress reports during the grant period, and future proposals. While rigorous conceptual planning and meticulous presentation are the converging themes in every section, the need for flexibility and adaptability is always emphasized to ensure that the individual needs of every research team and the uniqueness of every research idea are met.

Historically, there have been insufficient funds to sponsor all worthy research, but there was a time when, if not funded on the first try, a proposal could be expected to be successful after at most one or two revisions. However, given today's economic challenges and the challenges posed by emerging changes in the health care system that are bringing fewer patient-care dollars to support research and more researchers to the funding competition, the process has become significantly strained. In fact, some sponsors such as the National Institutes of Health are now precluding unlimited resubmissions of proposals—an unprecedented "three strikes and you're out" rule. Research funds in the system are earmarked for only the most outstanding proposals and, in many cases, for only a fraction of those ranked in this category. Therefore, successful grant-seekers must perform at the highest level at all stages of the process—from conception to presentation—to be competitive. The goal of this book is to provide the researcher in academic, clinical and business settings with the information needed to achieve this level of competitiveness.

Best wishes for success.

ACKNOWLEDGMENTS

My sincerest thanks to Harry Whitaker, Roch Lecours, and Mike Vannier, whose help was invaluable in getting this book off the ground; Gary Glover in the Department of Radiology at Stanford, for his unfailing support and mentoring, and for his contributions as a reader and interlocutor during the evolution of this work; to other members of the Department of Radiology and the Radiological Sciences Laboratory at Stanford, Herb Abrams, Tom Raffin, Bonnie Hale, Jessica Agramonte, and other colleagues, friends, and family at Stanford, in the Kings Mountain community, and elsewhere for encouragement, reviews of the manuscript, discussion, and lively debate; to my mother Ibolya Illes and my brother Leslie Illes—pillars in my life; to my children Adri and Kiah for their great patience and genuine enthusiasm for this project; and to my husband H. F. Machiel Van der Loos, with whose talent, intellect and love yet another big project in our life together is completed.

Although this work is based on many years of experience in project and program development, all names and examples contained herein are fictitious.

—Judy Illes

Chapter 1

Partners in the Funding Relationship

Successful, long-term research funding is grounded in the relationships that evolve explicitly between researchers and their sponsors and implicitly between researchers, sponsors, and society. Every strategic plan for achieving research funding must take into consideration these partners, their roles, and the interactions among them. A diagram of the overall funding process, in which research ideas—developed ideally within the context of a strategic plan—are translated into competitive proposals and ultimately into grant- or contract-funded research is shown in Fig. 1.1. The successful process explicitly unites a researcher, a host institution, and a proposal of significant scientific merit with a sponsor. The implicit link to society is the far-reaching benefit of scientific success.

ACADEMIC RESEARCHERS, CLINICAL RESEARCHERS, AND RESEARCH-ENTREPRENEURS

The first party in the relationship is the researcher: the basic sciences researcher in an academic or research institution; the clinician or physician scientist in an academic medical center; or the researcher-entrepreneur in the private business sector. In the United States today, there are more than 100,000 researchers in the brain and behavioral sciences representing a broad range of disciplines from education to neurology.

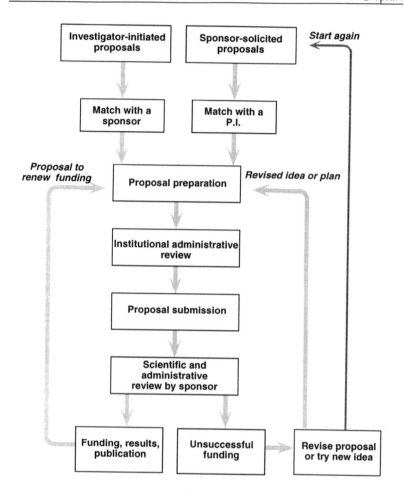

FIG. 1.1. Overview of the grants and contracts process.

Regardless of specific background, the researcher's role is to pursue new knowledge and information in the context of existing knowledge, with the object of at least incrementally enhancing the knowledge base in a particular domain. Science is thus advanced through ideas, proposals, funded research, results, and the dissemination of information. In the case of small businesses, science also yields a tangible commercial product.

During the 1960s and 1970s, researchers were considerably less susceptible to economic forces outside the academic or research institution than they are in the 1990s. Funding rates for basic research at that time were about 40%, renewal of a grant was a reasonable expectation, and many grants had a life cycle of 20 years or more. Steady scientific progress by a researcher was generally accompanied by a reasonable amount of dependable funding. The competition for funds in the 1990s is much more intense, however, and scientific merit must be accompanied not only by an underlying desire to make important contributions to society but, also, by skilled planning to enable it. The creation of a research funding plan, therefore, is an important step for a researcher at any point in a research career.

Figure 1.2 illustrates a systematic, albeit idealized, funding plan. As shown, the opportunities available either to the starting or to the experienced researcher are numerous. Each step in a funding plan should consider researcher eligibility in terms of career stage and type of opportunity, especially so that one opportunity does not preclude another (e.g., as in the case of a sponsor who will not fund a researcher who has already exceeded a certain threshold of support). Each step must also consider direct scientific and operational (e.g., personnel and equipment) needs. The outcome of each step will depend on the research timeline, progress, and results.

The execution of a funding plan draws the researcher into the world of sponsors. Sponsors are the researcher's target audience for ideas (expressed through proposals) and progress (expressed through regular reporting). For the researcher, selecting from among the many possible sponsors involves searching not only for a valid scientific match but, also, for a career match because the evolving, bilateral relationship can impact both the scientific direction of the research and the specialized professional circles to which the researcher belongs.

SPONSORS

Government Sponsors

Sponsors differ in configuration and size. They operate for the purpose of promoting progress in the areas that are important to them. In the United States, the federal government is the largest sponsor of basic research at research institutions and provides about 60% of the funding for those institutions. For health and medicine, the largest

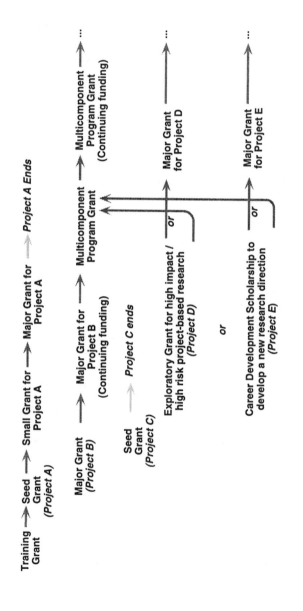

FIG. 1.2. Hypothetical long-term research funding plan and outcome. As a research program grows, parallel opportunities can be pursued strategically depending on the goals and success of the ongoing activities within the program.

government sponsor in the United States is the National Institutes of Health (NIH). NIH has approximately 30 institutes and centers representing widely varying interests and priorities. In 1998, for example, there are approximately 15,000 researchers funded by NIH, 2,000 reviewers, and hundreds of contexts in which health-related research is being pursued. This vast sponsor's budget is more than $12 billion, with target funding priority areas in AIDS, breast cancer, molecular imaging, and minority health.

The interests and priorities of other government agencies, both within and outside the United States, are equally broad and varied. For example, the U.S. National Science Foundation (NSF) provides overall support for education in science and engineering and for academic research infrastructure such as instrumentation and facilities modernization, especially as it applies to improving educational and training opportunities. Unlike NIH, whose purview is research for the improvement of health and health care, NSF's mission is to support the basic sciences. With a current budget of more than $3 billion, NSF supports almost 20,000 research and education projects in science and engineering (http://www.nsf.gov). In Canada, the major funding source for biomedical research is the Medical Research Council of Canada (MRC). With its $230 million budget, the MRC promotes basic and clinical research, as well as training of health scientists. Its counterpart, the Natural Sciences and Engineering Research Council of Canada (NSERC), is the national source of funding in science and technology, with more than 11,000 supported Canadian researchers (http://www.nserc.ca). In Europe, national agencies such as the Swiss Federal National Science Foundation (SNSF), promote research at academic and scientific institutions. The SNSF distributes 75% of its approximately $300 million budget and almost 2,500 grants in the areas of humanities and social sciences, mathematics, natural and engineering sciences, and biology and medicine (http://www.snsf.ch).

Nongovernment Sponsors

In contrast to government sponsors, nongovernment sponsors such as foundations have considerably smaller budgets and narrower areas of interest and priority. There are approximately 40,000 foundations in the

United States, divided into four types: independent, corporate, operating, and community foundations (Rich, 1996).

Independent Foundations.   Independent foundations are supported by individuals and families, and are operated either under the voluntary direction of the principals or by a board of trustees and professional staff. Areas of scientific interest for extramural support are predefined; geographical restrictions may also apply, depending on the foundation.

Corporate Foundations.   Corporate foundations, together with independent foundations, represent the large majority of the 40,000 foundations most commonly approached for extramural support. Corporate foundations are company sponsored, but are legally separate from them. Their funding activity is usually focused on research and education in areas related to the company's interests and to geographic areas in which the company has operations.

Operating Foundations.   Operating foundations are private foundations structured to fund their own intramural research, and are commonly found in the biomedical and pharmaceutical industries.

Community Foundations.   Community foundations are created to serve regional interests and priorities. This type of public entity receives its funds from a variety of donors, much like the independent foundations, and may support a broad range of research. However, distribution of funds extramurally is highly restricted to the region in which the foundation operates.

Much like the state of the geopolitical world today, in which countries come and go, sponsors—whether they are governmental or nongovernmental—form and disperse, separate and integrate. New ones appear each year, some may merge permanently with others or combine resources temporarily for specific programs, and some may run out of money. For example, the NIH established an Institute for Alternative Medicine in the early 1990s; NSF and the Whitaker Foundation joined together in 1994 to support a research initiative on cost-effective health care technology. In parallel with these new initiatives, the federal Office of Technology Licensing, for example, was abolished and the U.S. superconducting collider project was terminated. Therefore, knowing which sponsors are in a formative or sunset phase, and which sponsors have funds to disperse or none remaining, can be valuable data points in finding a funding match.

Accessing Information About Sponsors

Information about sponsors' standing interests and regional giving priorities can be obtained through their regular publications, annual reports, and home pages on the Internet. The Foundation Center Directory and associated publications also provide comprehensive summaries of sponsors spanning all disciplines (http://www.fdncenter.org). The American Psychological Association (APA) publishes a compendium of funding sources specifically for the brain and behavioral sciences (Herring, 1994).

Many sponsors also have changing priorities that appear in the form of special announcements, program announcements, or as requests for applications (RFAs) and requests for proposals (RFPs).

Special announcements, program announcements, and RFAs alert the scientific community about a new or renewed interest of a sponsor in a priority or expanding area. These opportunities can have an extended life span, and proposals may be submitted for any published deadline until the opportunity is withdrawn. The availability of funds, however, is not a precondition to their release.

By contrast, RFPs signify the specific availability of funds either for a grant or for a contract in a well-defined research area. Availability of RFP funding for a grant, per se, implies that a sponsor is seeking to fund research in a specific area, with the approach to the research proposed by the applicant. Contract funding, however, is typically for research with goals and deliverables explicitly directed by the sponsor. The applicant must be responsive to the contract terms with a time line for work and budget that conforms to the sponsor's specific criteria. The impending release of an RFP is usually announced 3 to 4 months in advance of its publication. Once the RFP is released the required time to respond may be as short as 45 to 90 days and, unlike RFAs, it is usually a one-time solicitation.

Both RFAs and RFPs specify the type of funding mechanisms that may be used. The most common mechanisms across sponsors—both governmental and nongovernmental—are project-based research grants, multicomponent research program grants, career development grants, and small business grants. These are the focus of chapters 2 through 5. Other less frequently utilized mechanisms, such as construction and instrumentation grants, are also discussed in chapter 3 on multicomponent programs.

Institutional-sponsored projects and research development offices learn about these special funding opportunities through regular hard copy and electronic announcements. These come from sponsors locally, nationally (like NIH), and internationally, and are now accessible to every individual who has access to the World Wide Web. The Web has also provided access to funding information through sites maintained by professional societies such as the American Psychological Association (http://www.apa.org/science/fbinfo.html), the American Academy of Neurology (http://www.aan.com/public_res/publicfunding.html), the Society for Neuroscience (http://www.sfn.org/agency), and the Radiological Society of North America (http://www.rsna.org) (see also Bergan, 1996, for tips on electronically accessing sponsor information).

Many services also exist as central distributors of funding information. Some services, such as the Medical Research Funding Bulletin (Science Support Center, New York) and the ARIS Funding Reports (http://www.arisnet.com), have subscription charges. A new Community of Science, Inc. service is designed to meet the information needs of research and development researchers worldwide, and is also a subscription-based resource (http://medoc.gdb.org/repos/fund). Others, such as the FEDIX (alert@zappa.fie.com) e-mail information service, are free of charge. FEDIX electronically distributes information about government research and educational funding opportunities at no charge to FEDIX subscribers. Distribution is made on the basis of a match between key words provided by the subscriber and participating agencies. Participating agencies include the Department of Energy, Federal Aviation Administration, NASA, Office of Naval Research, Air Force Office of Research, National Science Foundation, NIH, and the Department of Education. Distribution is daily.

New funding information sources are appearing routinely in the age of rapid electronic information dissemination; at the time of this writing, one of the latest and most promising one-stop shopping services specifically for training and early faculty development is Grantsnet (http://www.grantsnet.org), sponsored by the American Association for the Advancement of Sciences and the Howard Hughes Medical Institute.

It is not uncommon to subscribe to multiple sources of funding information. Although there is a fair amount of redundancy between the services, with as much as 25% to 30% new information in each, the time invested in proactively perusing them is worthwhile.

Funding Power, Paylines, and Award Rates

Funding power is the level at which a sponsor will fund proposals and, even with the most well-managed assets, it would be exceptional that a sponsor could fund every proposal submitted to it. Therefore, although scientific review determines which proposals are meritorious, a payline determines which proposals can actually be funded from that group. Paylines are the funding cutoffs defined either as an absolute score (e.g., a score on a scale of 1 to 100) or as relative score (e.g., percentile) or rank (e.g., 6th of 92 proposals) that indicate the position of a proposal with respect to other proposals reviewed in that cycle or over a set of cycles (the advantage of averaging over a series of cycles is that it tends to correct for some inevitable variability that exists between reviewers and review groups).

Sponsor paylines may be set a priori, as in the case when a sponsor funds only, for example, ten proposals in any cycle regardless of cost or number of proposals received, or may be set on the basis of the trade-off between available funds and the total cost of the most meritorious proposals. Although the latter is the norm, it is important when developing a research plan, to focus on the science foremost, and to let the science drive the formula for an accurate and representative budget. The reverse equation usually yields a scientifically compromised proposal and rarely yields a successful funding result.

Paylines for RFAs and RFPs are usually consistent with the overall funding history of a sponsor, although it is a common misconception that the competition for funding will be less in response to an RFA or

RFP than for an unsolicited proposal initiated by the investigator. In reality, however, because RFAs and RFPs often have the effect of stimulating new ideas and research directions, there are often so many responses to an RFA or RFP that the award rate (i.e., the percent of proposals actually funded) may be a smaller fraction than usual. It is important, therefore, to resist digression from a well-developed funding plan to respond to an unexpected solicitation unless the opportunity is truly a good one. The conceptualization pathways presented in the following chapters are designed to maximize the selection of good matches and to triage the potentially weaker ones.

SOCIETY AS THE BENEFACTOR OF RESEARCH

The third partner in the research relationship is society—the global community—that must itself be considered with respect to its component scientific and nonscientific arms.

The scientific community is as much the recipient of research results as it is a monitor of it. The relationship is in fact circular: Scientific ideas lead to research proposals, research proposals lead to funding, funding leads to results, results lead to publications and new research, and so on. The scientific community measures the researcher on success at each of these points, and advancement and opportunity to continue in this cycle is contingent on such success. This interplay exists within the peer review process for grants as it does in peer review for publications.

The nonscientific community also has a great impact on the priorities and directions of research in the world today. Through the efforts of lobbyists and activists and through the interests of generous philanthropists, the nonscientific community can strongly influence the priority areas of the government and nongovernment sponsors. As a single example, more high-impact, high-visibility health-related research involving underserved populations is being conducted in the late 1990s than ever before.

There is often resistance to the influence that the nonscientific community has on research policy, but this arm of society is an important partner and gatekeeper to the directions that modern research takes. In fact, government and nongovernment sponsors alike, and virtually all institutional human review and animal review boards, include members of both the scientific and nonscientific communities to provide balance and complementary perspective to the many decisions about research that must be made each day.

SUMMARY

Improved knowledge about the brain and behavior, novel ideas in alternative medicine, just like new emerging forms of art and music, benefit all people regardless of whether they belong to the scientific or nonscientific community. The relationship and interplay between the partners in the funding relationship, and the manner that research ideas take this relationship into consideration and build on it, underlie the fundamental elements of good, proposable research ideas.

Chapter 2

Project-Based Research

Project-based research consists of a single focused study or a unified set of studies that may be driven by hypotheses and experiments, or goals and tasks. Depending on the various considerations discussed here, project-based research may be best accomplished by a feasibility seed study that is of limited scope, by an exploratory study that is intrinsically risky, or by a full-scale effort. Regardless of the scale, however, the project should form an integral part of an overall research program, and benefit from a history and foundation of work that has a significant life cycle.

DETERMINING PROJECT SCALE: FULL-SCALE, EXPLORATORY, AND SEED RESEARCH

Four interdependent criteria may be defined for determining the scale at which a research project should be pursued: attributes of the preliminary data, budgetary requirements, anticipated impact of the results, and opportunity (see Table 2.1).

Attributes of the Preliminary Data

The first criteria in determining project scale are the amount and strength of data that exist in favor of the project. For exploratory studies, which are risky and innovative by definition, there must be some preliminary evidence of feasibility and merit. The evidence may be only indirectly related to the project at hand and may be drawn from outside and within

TABLE 2.1

Summary Parameters and Criteria for Seed, Exploratory, and Full-Scale Research Projects

	Seed Projects	Exploratory Projects	Full-Scale Projects
Attributes of the preliminary data	Little preliminary data exist for the project.	The project is risky or represents a new direction in an overall research program.	Data from within the laboratory exist as proof of concept for the project.
		Sufficient data exist from within the laboratory and potentially from outside to justify further testing but do not provide proof for the concept.	The preliminary data have been collected in a rigorous way.
		Existing data have not necessarily been collected in a rigorous way.	

(Continues)

TABLE 2.1 (Continued)

	Seed Projects	Exploratoyr Projects	Full-Scale Projects
Budgetary requirements	The project can be accomplished on a limited budget (e.g., $50,000 per year or less) and in a relatively short period of time (up to 2 years).	The project can be accomplished on a limited budget and in a relatively short period of time (up to 2 years).	The project may require a full scale budget and take several years to complete.
Anticipated robustness of the results	Completion of the project will provide proof of concept and data for full-scale funding.	Completion of the project will provide proof of concept and data for full-scale funding.	Completion of the project will yield conclusive results.

the researcher's own laboratory (where some preliminary work must have been done, even for the most exploratory projects).

By contrast, seed and full-scale projects should be supported largely, if not entirely, by data that are directly relevant to the project under development and should be generated by the researcher's laboratory. The attributes of existing data from within a laboratory, then, are the first moderating factors in deciding between a seed project or a full-scale effort.

Budgetary Requirements

The second set of criteria for determining project scale consists of the budget needed to carry out the work and the time needed to do it. Seed and exploratory projects are typically capped at budgets of less than $100,000 per year in direct costs for research (i.e., exclusive of institutional overhead, also referred to as *indirect costs*), for 1 or 2 years. The budgetary range for full-scale projects is considerably greater, potentially reaching several hundreds of thousands of dollars per year with large sponsors, for as many as 5 years.

Anticipated Impact of the Results

The third criterion in determining whether a project should be developed on a seed, exploratory, or full-scale basis is the potential impact of the results. For example, if the results can be expected to have a significant impact in a discipline and withstand the scrutiny of peer review in publication, then the criterion for a full-scale effort is met. By contrast, if the outcome of the research can realistically be expected to provide only proof of concept or feasibility data for future work (as in the case when the data would be sufficient to reveal trends but too limited to yield statistical significance), it does not meet the stand-alone criterion, and the pursuit of a full-scale effort would be premature.

Opportunity

Determining project scale should be based on an assessment of the trade-offs between the internal variables—attributes of the preliminary data and intrinsic riskiness of the work or new direction, budgetary requirements, and expected results—versus external factors such as the availability of set-aside funding by a sponsor. The existence of set-aside funds for a given project scale can be captivating, but an opportunity should only be pursued if the trade-offs are favorable. For example, an announcement of an opportunity may be issued for exploratory research in the neurological sciences, with the goal of specifically seeding new research for which another funding mechanism does not exist. On the one hand, it may be an ideal opportunity for a researcher to launch a project based on data that have been accumulated anecdotally in another study. On the other hand, it would not be an appropriate opportunity for a project that is neither risky nor exploratory and for which gathering sufficient data for full-scale funding is only a matter of time and not a matter of science.

CONCEPTUALIZING PROJECT-BASED RESEARCH

The process for developing project-based research, irrespective of project scale, and testing for competitiveness is stepwise but not discrete. As the conceptualization pathway illustrates (Fig. 2.1) the process is iterative and, as one decision is taken, each of the other decisions in the process is likely to be affected. The 10 critical decisions are discussed in detail here.

The Idea Should Be Grounded in Science

Successful ideas emerge from previous ideas and resulting data or experience. The strongest foundation is achieved through the work of others, in combination with the previous results of the proposing research team, and some preliminary work to determine feasibility. Successfully funded ideas typically do not emerge from an idea that does not have at least some scientific roots, regardless of how intuitive that idea may be. Purely anecdotal observation, life experience, or a feeling that something will work do not provide an appropriate or strong foundation for a project. This is not to say that creativity and innovation are discouraged, by any means. On the contrary, creativity and innovation are highly valued in the context of an established body of knowledge. But, at this first decision in the conceptualization pathway, scientific foundation is essential.

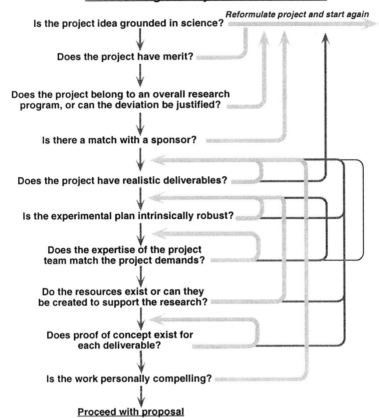

Given an idea for a research project composed of either a single study or a set of studies:

Reformulate project and start again

Is the project idea grounded in science?

Does the project have merit?

Does the project belong to an overall research program, or can the deviation be justified?

Is there a match with a sponsor?

Does the project have realistic deliverables?

Is the experimental plan intrinsically robust?

Does the expertise of the project team match the project demands?

Do the resources exist or can they be created to support the research?

Does proof of concept exist for each deliverable?

Is the work personally compelling?

Proceed with proposal

FIG. 2.1. Conceptualization pathway for project-based research. In this pathway, as in all subsequent pathways, the descending arrows show the progression from one decision to the next. Horizontal arrows point to the first-choice iteration if immediate continuation to the next decision is not advisable, and to further alternatives from left to right, as needed.

The Idea Must Have Merit

Merit may be defined in terms of both need and impact. The definition takes into consideration all the parties in the research relationship.

Need.   Need may be measured by the effect that an existing condition has on the scientific community, society, or both. Need may be defined objectively, for example, by a measurement of the number of people affected by a disease for which there is no cure, or subjectively by the importance of advancing knowledge about a physiological or physical system for the understanding of human behavior.

Impact. Impact may also be measured using both quantitative and subjective metrics. For example, the net effect that a new treatment may have on patient survival, time to return to the workplace, or on health care costs to society are well-defined variables that can be evaluated objectively. The subjective counterpart resides in the extent to which the research systematically moves a field forward from the existing knowledge base. The net change that a result brings to a knowledge base and the outcome thereof (i.e., the future work it stimulates), is the *subjective impact.*

When considering the question of merit, both need and impact should be well matched to a potential sponsor. For example, if a sponsor has specified that exploring new ways to remediate dyslexia in elementary school children is its priority, then research on preschool children should not be proposed, no matter how intrinsically meritorious the research may be. The research envelope can be stretched to justify a match, but it is important to bear in mind that the likelihood of funding success is directly correlated with the reality and robustness of the match.

At this point in the pathway, questions about need and impact should be addressed separately. Four combinations are then possible (summarized in Table 2.2).

1.   The query leads to the conclusion that the project responds to a significant need and, if successful, will have a significant impact. This is the ideal situation, and the researcher should continue to the next decision in the pathway.

2.   The query leads to the conclusion that the need is limited but the impact is potentially high. Take, for example, the case of Tourette's syndrome, which affects a relatively limited population, but for whom the development of effective pharmacotherapy with no side effects will have a great impact in terms of patient quality of life: The project passes the test of merit. If the impact measurably extends to the global community in terms of patient independence and reduced health care costs, for example, then the merit criterion is met with even greater confidence.

TABLE 2.2
Testing the Merit of a Research Idea for Competitiveness

Need	Impact	Action
High	High	Proceed to next decision.
Low	High	Proceed to next decision (but this may be risky) or consider an iteration to increase need.
High	Low	Reformulate and reevaluate beginning at Decision 1 in the pathway.
Low or none	Low or none	Reformulate and reevaluate beginning at Decision 1 in the pathway.

3.   Both need and impact appear to be low. In this case, reformulating the project and reevaluating its merit would be the most proactive way to proceed. Reformulation need not change the idea underlying the research dramatically; however, at least one of the merit criteria should be significantly met for the project to be competitive.

4.   If the query yields a realization that there is truly no need for an idea to be pursued as a research project, then there is likely to be no impact. Although the project may be enjoyable to carry out, from a funding point of view it would best be abandoned in favor of one that is potentially more fruitful.

The Project Should Relate to an Overall Program

The next criterion has to do with whether the project relates to an overall goal. The most competitive research projects are developed in the context of a research program that is defined by a broad and potentially multifaceted goal. The most competitive projects are also unified conceptually across sponsors, and connected longitudinally over time. Even projects that represent a new direction for a researcher should be linked logically to an existing professional history and set of overall goals. Projects that are developed in either a scientific or professional vacuum do not tend to do well in the funding arena.

A project that is a follow-up to an ongoing one should be logically continuous; not necessarily a direct continuation per se, but a natural extension (see also chapter 11). If it is not a natural extension, then its credibility as continuing work will be questionable and its fundability will be jeopardized. In such a case, the alternative of developing the research in the context of an entirely new proposal should be considered.

When testing for competitiveness, therefore, the query at this point is whether the project idea is well integrated into an overall program from the point of view of both the problem area and the scientific approach. It is entirely reasonable to cross into a new field—the problem area—with a promising technique—the scientific approach—or to try a new technique in an established research area. However, even for the most exploratory project, the researcher must have some relevant experience to be seriously competitive. If not, the researcher should either coordinate with someone who has the appropriate expertise, or reformulate the project to bring it in from afield. When mandated, reformulation should begin at the first decision.

A Good Match With a Sponsor Must Exist

It is essential to be cognizant of possible sponsors throughout the entire research development process, and test the sponsor-related considerations for the first time at this point in the pathway. These considerations are the trade-off between aspects of the idea being developed, the sponsor's interests and priorities, and what, in terms of funds, the sponsor will be able to do for the researcher. For example, in the case of a health-related project that will impact hundreds of thousands of people per year, will take a minimum of 3 years to carry out, and will require a substantial budget, the National Institutes of Health would be an appropriate target sponsor. By contrast, a small project that will have a significant impact on a small number of people may be more successfully funded by a special interest foundation.

Thus, two questions should be addressed at this point:

1. Can a sponsor be identified who will share an interest in the project?
2. Can that sponsor provide the necessary level of funding to carry out the work?

The answer to both these questions should be affirmative because if there is no match, there will be no prospect for funding. Ideally more than one sponsor will meet both criteria. In this case, the decision to choose a particular sponsor will have to be based on the funding history of all prospective sponsors (i.e., by inspection of the list of previously funded projects), on the sponsors' paylines, and on dialogue with program managers who can provide an understanding of how close or far the project is to meeting their short- or long-term goals.

The Project Must Have Realistic Deliverables

Deliverables are the core results of the work on which the success or failure of the project is measured. The deliverables should be specific, focused, and linked rationally to one another. They must comprise a unit that ultimately yields the achievement of a specific overall goal.

Two types of deliverables may exist, consistent with the concepts of hypothesis-driven and development-driven research.

Hypothesis-Driven Deliverables. Hypothesis-driven deliverables are derived from experiments designed to test predictions about the behavior of one condition compared to or in relation with other conditions, including possibly a known condition or gold standard. The experiments should be designed to test the predictions statistically, with enough rigor (i.e., experimental control) and power (i.e., data) that the results can be interpreted meaningfully.

Development-Driven Deliverables. Deliverables in development- or goal-driven research are the creation, discovery, or optimization of techniques, methods, or products. Whereas statistical tests provide the parameters for hypothesis-driven deliverables, other external measures can exist for development-driven research. These measures, as the researcher conceives of them, are the endpoints of the tasks associated with the deliverables. The conceptualization process for development-driven deliverables may be less constrained, but subject to greater scrutiny. In the development of a new device, for example, a set of endpoints may be the determination of the best materials and design for manufacturing a prototype. In the development of a new clinical protocol to evaluate personality disorders, a set of endpoints may be the determination of acceptable test duration and the selection of a written or oral modality for its administration. However, whether these are suitable and sufficient endpoints in the context of a larger overall goal is a subjective matter. Therefore, endpoints should be especially well-defined, and justified against both a time line and a budget.

The juxtaposition of both hypothesis-driven and goal-driven deliverables into a single project is definitely a viable strategy and can provide effective and elegant solutions to scientific query.

When testing for competitiveness at this point in the pathway, the answer to each of the following questions should be affirmative.

1. Does the set of deliverables support an overall project goal?
2. Are the deliverables logically linked in a scientific way to one another?
3. Are the deliverables logically linked in a pragmatic way to one another? For example, is the chronology of deliverables reasonable and efficient?
4. Will each deliverable yield a meaningful result or significant step toward the accomplishment of the project goal?

If the query does not yield positive answers to each of these questions, the deliverables should be reformulated. The deliverables to which the query yielded a negative response should first be addressed individually. Then, the new set of deliverables should be re-evaluated in its entirety.

The Experimental Plan Should Be Sound

Development of the experimental plan must conform entirely to the projected deliverables. For each deliverable, there should be:

- A study or set of studies for which there is a hypothesis or development objective.
- A rationale.
- A rational procedure or set of procedures.
- A means of data analysis and a method for interpreting the results.
- A means of dealing with experimental limitations or unexpected obstacles.
- An anticipated significance.

Hypothesis or Development Objective. A testable hypothesis or measurable development goal should be associated with every study that is proposed. Hypotheses should be focused on variables; development objectives on endpoints.

Rationale. The rationale for a project should be based on both the successes and failures of previous work. The failures give further evidence of need; the successes give evidence of the potential pay-offs of further exploration. The rationale should also address the choice of an approach to the research (i.e., the motivation for proceeding one way instead of another), but should not deal with the need or impact, which are considered under merit.

Procedures and Analyses. The procedures are the unequivocally rigorous steps taken in execution of the research plan. Each step in the procedures should be feasible, justifiable, and best-suited to the efficient delivery of results. For example, there should be a clearly described means of recruiting appropriate and sufficient numbers of subjects for a project that involves the use of human subjects. As another example, if the procedure requires the use of a unique animal model that is available only from a secondary laboratory, then every aspect of collaboration with that laboratory should be feasible. There should be a sufficient budget to cover the costs that the outside laboratory will incur including, for example, the cost of transportation to the primary research site. In addition, the cooperation must pass the test of reasonableness (e.g., that the animals can be transported safely and economically).

Another important test of rigor is the logical continuity and precision of experimental variables. Variables such as drug dosages should be based on scientific reasoning or actual usage data, and administered in increments that can be justified explicitly. If data are acquired in different modalities, such as different imaging modalities, then they should be acquired in a way that will allow direct comparison or utilization as effective components in the overall plan.

Both the approach to data collection and the means of data analysis must carefully follow the stated hypotheses and development objectives. It is not uncommon for a proposal to return to a researcher unfunded, with the criticism that although both the deliverables and procedures were worthy, the procedures as proposed would not produce the result promised by the deliverables.

Experimental Limitations and Obstacles.   An important part of any research project is the appreciation of not only what it will deliver, but also what it will not. Obstacles should be anticipated, and there should be procedures to overcome them. This may be accomplished by using an alternate methodological approach or by collecting additional data. If there are limitations to the project, then the manner in which the limitations affect the clarity and significance of the results should be considered. Limitations are acceptable provided they do not fatally compromise the usefulness of the results and can be resolved by further work.

Once an initial experimental plan is drafted, it should be reviewed objectively for its overall cohesiveness and its potential to meet the objectives of the overall goal. Before proceeding to the next decision in the pathway, the answers to the following questions should all be affirmative:

1. Does the research have a driving hypothesis or development objective for each deliverable?
2. Is the rationale for each deliverable justified?
3. Are the experimental procedures scientifically rigorous and constructed in a way that they can be tested to yield meaningful results?
4. Can the limitations of the proposed work be addressed, and does a plan exist for dealing with unexpected findings and obstacles?

If the answers are not all affirmative, then the experimental plan should be revised or the deliverables revisited until this is achieved.

The Expertise of the Research Team
Must Match the Project Goals

Once the vision for a project has been established and the deliverables and scientific plan formulated, a research team needs to be assembled. The research team may be formed from existing members of a laboratory or clinical group or supplemented by other researchers from outside who bring special skills to the project. The research team should comprise people who possess expertise to carry out the work, bring cohesiveness to the group as defined by skills that are complementary but not redundant, and are able to work together to fulfill the desired goals.

Whether the research team is organized in a vertical, multilayered, hierarchical way with few people at each of many levels, or in a lateral organization with several people at fewer levels, the functional roles of each member of the research team will need to be defined explicitly.

The principals of the research team are the core members who have an overall investment in the results of the work, have responsibility for specific aspects of it, and who benefit from the outcome either in academic currency—publications and presentations—or financially from its success, in the case where a product is developed. In descending order of degree of responsibility, core personnel may be principal investigators (PI), co-principal investigators (co-PI), investigators, or collaborators (Table 2.3). The non-core personnel such as research assistants, technologists and technicians are expected to have specific roles to play, but should not have responsibilities for the project that extend beyond their specific functions. Entitlement to publications is not necessarily a given for non-core personnel, and should be decided in advance of the work to be carried out.

Core Personnel

Principal Investigator.   The principal investigator (PI) will have primary responsibility for both the scientific and administrative execution of the work. Generally, the PI is also the individual who conceived of the project, but if his or her expertise or seniority

TABLE 2.3

Summary of the Roles of Core Personnel

Core Personnel	Selection Criteria
Principal investigator	Conceived of the project or program.
	Has overall responsibility for scientific and administrative aspects of the work.
Co-principal investigator	Possibly co-conceived of the project idea.
	Provides key expertise and seniority not represented by the PI, and additional administrative oversight.
	Has the secondary responsibility for overseeing the scientific progress of the work.
Investigator	Participated in the formulation of the scientific plan.
	Is invested in all aspects of the outcome of the work.
Collaborator	Is invested in certain aspects of the work, and brings specific expertise in these areas.

do not match the specific aims or magnitude of the project that ultimately evolve for the work, then a co-PI should be selected with whom the principal responsibility for the work can be shared (see also next section). As two examples, a co-PIship may occur when bench-top engineering or laboratory studies led by one PI precede testing in the clinical environment led by a co-PI, or when a relatively junior investigator is in a key position to lead a multicomponent program as a PI (see chapter 4), but requires a co-PI to supply additional academic and administrative experience.

Co-Principal Investigator. A co-PI, if needed, should be designated on a project to share responsibilities for the overall conduct of the research proposed, or if the project has multiple major components that cannot reasonably be represented by the expertise of a single individual, as described previously.

Investigators. Project investigators are independent researchers who are vested professionally in the outcome of the research and whose expertise is key to the success of the work. The choice of investigators should be made on the basis of the specific requirements of the work proposed, and their effort allocated to a project should be driven by the responsibilities associated with those requirements.

Collaborators. Collaborators are individuals within the PI's organization who play a very specific role on a project and have an interest in the outcome of the work. They may, for example, refer patients to a study, provide statistical assistance to the project, or offer special expertise that is necessary for the interpretation of the data.

Non-Core Personnel

Professional Personnel. There is a wide range of professional personnel who provide scientific, technical, and administrative support to a project. Their effort is related to specific functions on a project and should be budgeted accordingly. Their level of expertise and their level of involvement should determine whether they are core or non-core personnel.

Research Associates and Assistants. Staff research associates and research assistants provide valuable support to a project by virtue of their specialized training and interest. Funding for associates and assistants is an easily accepted budget item provided that the science supports it. They should be chosen and budgeted for carefully.

Students. Predoctoral and postdoctoral students both provide valuable input to a project and benefit from the training associated with it. In addition to the actual work done on a project, postdoctoral students may also help supervise the work of predoctoral students. The designation of postdoctoral fellows as key personnel is dependent on their experience and level of expertise. Graduate students are generally not regarded as key personnel.

Consultants. Consultants bring very specific expertise to a project, and have a limited commitment to the project overall. Consultants may be drawn from within an organization or from the outside.

Given these parameters, the answers to the following questions must be affirmative before proceeding to the next decision in the pathway:

1. Does the PI possess the appropriate expertise to oversee the project?
2. Do the team members collectively represent the expertise needed to carry out the work proposed?
3. Are the expectations of all the investigators justified by the science to be done?
4. Is the support to be provided by non-core personnel sufficient given the project goals?
5. Is the group cohesive, ideally with a previous track record of successful collaboration?

In the event that one or more of the answers is not affirmative, a first pass at reformulating the team should be made. If the answers are still not all affirmative, the pathway should be revisited at the deliverables step—the fifth decision—and iterated until a perfect match occurs.

The Proper Resources Must Exist or Become Available

Resources include the overall research environment in terms of the facilities and the instrumentation and tools contained therein. The facilities include all the space that may be required to carry out the work. There should be sufficient laboratory space, office space, and so forth to accommodate the work proposed and the people needed to carry it out.

Even the best formulated project will have little chance of success if the tools available to the research team are limited, outdated, or not available at the level mandated by the research plan. For example, if a project will require regular inpatient magnetic resonance imaging, there should be sufficient time available on a busy hospital scanner for the scans to be obtained. If specialized tools are needed, there should be sufficient room in the budget for their purchase or loan. The option chosen should be clearly described when translating the idea into a written proposal.

The single critical query at this point, therefore is:

1. Do the resources exist or can they be acquired to carry out the work?

If the answer is negative and irreversibly so, the experimental plan should be reformulated at the level of the sixth decision or the deliverables revisited at the level of the fifth decision until the match is complete.

Proof of Concept

One of the last considerations in the conceptualization pathway for project-based research is proof of concept, first and foremost the quality of the preliminary data or prior data available in support of the idea. With some relaxation of the following criteria for seed and exploratory projects, the data should be complete and convincing from two points of view:

1. The data must demonstrate that the project, as conceptualized, is likely to yield meaningful results. Therefore, the compendium of data must provide meaningful information, even if it actually may only lead to the need for further research.

2. The data must convey the feasibility of each deliverable, both in terms of the intrinsic feasibility of the underlying idea, and in terms of the capabilities to deliver each as promised.

Implied at the proof of concept step, as well, is that the idea and the approach taken to study it are inventive and compelling. Inventiveness is measured by the uniqueness of an approach to a problem, with a strong supporting rationale. The approach is further compelling when the inventiveness is well matched with efficiency and promises to reveal a previously elusive phenomenon.

The queries at this point are, therefore:

1. Do the preliminary data support the overall project idea?
2. Do the preliminary data support each project deliverable?
3. Do the preliminary data demonstrate that this project and the expected results will stand out among others in both the scientific and world communities?

Should the answer to Query 1 be negative, the entire approach should be re-evaluated, with potentially new data collection as a consequence. Should the answer to Query 2 be negative, more data for the given or revised deliverables should be acquired. Should the answer to the third query be negative, all aspects of the project should be re-evaluated according to the following new set of questions:

1. Does the project idea need to be reformulated to become more compelling? If so, reconsider the merit of the project and re-evaluate beginning at the level of the second decision.
2. Do some or all of the project deliverables need to be reformulated? If so, revisit the deliverables at the level of the fifth decision.
3. Does the scientific approach need to be reconfigured? If so, revisit the experimental plan at the level of the sixth decision.

Through iterations in the pathway, affirmative answers to these queries will ultimately be achieved, and the project idea can confidently be turned into a project proposal.

The Research Should be Personally Compelling

Regardless of how much time is expended in conceptualizing a project idea, the final decision is the reality check that queries whether you are passionate about the idea that has been developed. It is difficult to convey passion about an idea in a proposal and to convince reviewers of your determination to carry out the work if that determination does not exist. Therefore, proceed to writing only if this criterion is met. Otherwise, beginning at the level of the deliverables, evaluate where the idea breaks down in terms of personal desirability. Is it a breakdown, for example, in the science or in the people? Then reformulate and re-evaluate.

SUMMARY

Three approaches to project-based research have been discussed: small-scale seed and exploratory research and full-scale projects. The critical common decisions in the conceptualization pathway are summarized in Table 2.4.

Although it would be desirable to have a relative weighting for the importance of each of these elements, it would not be realistic. The relative value of each element will depend on the project and, simply stated, the elements are all essential and interdependent for success.

TABLE 2.4
Summary of the Critical Decisions and Key Features
in Conceptualizing Project-Based Research

Critical Decisions	Key Features
Scientific groundedness	Project idea emerges from a scientific knowledge base.
Merit	Project idea represents both current need and eventual impact.
Program fit	Project idea is a discrete step in overall research program.
Match with a sponsor	Priority area and budget are met by at least one sponsor.
Deliverables	Each deliverable yields a result; the set of results yields the project goal.
Experimental plan	Scientific approach is sufficiently rigorous to achieve predicted results and to deal with unexpected obstacles.
Research team	Expertise covers the scientific requirements of the project; the team is cohesive and has a track record of collaboration.
Resources	State-of-the-art facilities and instrumentation are available and accessible.
Proof of concept	Preliminary data demonstrate project feasibility and innovation.
Reality check	PI is personally interested in carrying out the research.

Chapter 3

Career Development Programs

Securing a career development award is often one of the first major steps in the development of an overall research program. It is the opportunity for a researcher to acquire independence, identify a scientific niche and become a contributor to it, and gain the experience needed to become competitive for future major funding. In this chapter, the term *career development* is used broadly to encapsulate training scholarships as well as faculty/scientist career awards.

MECHANISMS OF SUPPORT FOR TRAINING AND CAREER DEVELOPMENT

Table 3.1 provides the matrix of the many mechanisms available to support career development and associated goals, and forms the basis for the ensuing discussion.

CONCEPTUALIZING TRAINING AND CAREER DEVELOPMENT PROGRAMS

The root structure of a successful career development program consists of an overall training goal, strong mentorship, a strong research environment, a solid research project, and a well-matched sponsor. These roots form the basis of the conceptualization pathway shown in Fig. 3.1.

TABLE 3.1

Features of Postdoctoral, Scholarship, and Career Development Training Programs

Program Types	Eligibility	Goal	Mentor	Laboratory
Postdoctoral training fellowships	Postdoctoral fellows	Expand or refine existing research experience. Shift into a related but different area of research.	Mentor required.	Independent laboratory is not expected.
Scholarships	Postdoctoral fellows or early career researchers	Expand or refine existing research experience. Establish a definitive role as expert in an area.	Mentor required for postdoctoral fellow scholars, and usually required for early career researchers (even when not required, per se, a collaborating or consulting mentor is advisable).	Independent laboratory is expected for early career researchers.
Career development awards	Early career researchers; senior researchers	Establish a definitive role as an expert in an area.	Mentor may not be required, but having a collaborating or consulting mentor is always advisable.	Independent laboratory is expected.

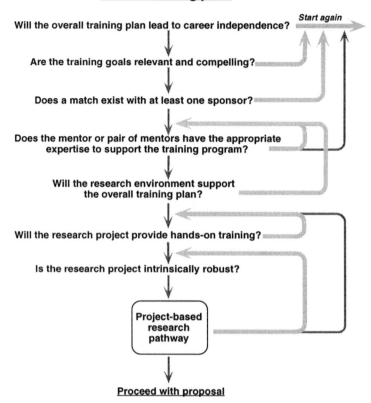

Given a training plan:

Will the overall training plan lead to career independence?

Are the training goals relevant and compelling?

Does a match exist with at least one sponsor?

Does the mentor or pair of mentors have the appropriate expertise to support the training program?

Will the research environment support the overall training plan?

Will the research project provide hands-on training?

Is the research project intrinsically robust?

Project-based research pathway

Proceed with proposal

FIG. 3.1. Conceptualization pathway for career development programs.

The Training Plan Should Lead to Career Independence

The first decision in the conceptualization pathway for career development funding considers plans for the eventual independence of the researcher and prospects for employment in the marketplace. Future independence is derived from the overall quality of the training program, and can be characterized by several well-defined metrics such as the ability to conceptualize an overall research program, plan and carry out component research projects independently, train and mentor other researchers, and compete successfully for funding. Therefore, the plan should encompass training in a broad range of skills, including program planning, refinement of laboratory skills, teaching, and grant writing.

When prospective training is not contiguous with previous training but marks a career change, the plan must also take into account the motivation for and suitability of the change. These are subjective issues, however, for which strict rules and guidelines do not apply. For example, a career change may be motivated by a shift in interest from one cognitive area such as language to another such as memory, from one disease area such as stroke to another such as neurodegenerative disease, or from one technology modality such as positron emission tomography (PET) to another such as functional magnetic resonance imaging (fMRI). Such changes would not require much justification, particularly when driven by research results acquired during ongoing work and the desire to extend them into other domains. However, a particularly strong rationale would be needed to justify the need for a new, eventually independent researcher who originates from an unrelated discipline. In addition, the overall training plan would need enough depth and rigor that it could realistically yield independence and competitiveness in a relatively short period of time.

With these considerations in mind, the answers to the following questions must be affirmative before continuing on to the next decision in the pathway:

1. Will the program yield specialization in a niche in which the potential for growth and advancement exists?

In addition, if the program marks a career change, then:

2. Is the change justifiable in terms of the factors that motivate it and in terms of the degree to which it represents a deviation from previous training?

If the answers to these queries are not affirmative, funding will be difficult to acquire and a new training direction should be considered.

The Training Goals Must be Relevant and Compelling

Regardless of how well the components of a training package are conceptualized, if there is no need for the type of expert it will yield, if the expertise is very broad, or if the marketplace is already saturated, it is unlikely there will be a sponsor who will be interested in investing in it. It is imperative, therefore, that the training plan will yield a researcher who has specialized skills that can be supported both by the relevant professional field and by the funding environment, and whose work in the short- and long-term will serve the needs of society.

A Good Match With a Sponsor Should Exist

The central query at this point concerns the researcher as an individual. The query considers research interest, years of training, gender, minority group, and special interests.

Some sponsors have hard criteria for training support and may fund, for example, only women in medicine in first-time academic appointments. The criteria of many other sponsors are broader, in that they have preferences for certain types of researchers but are not, in principle, exclusive of any researcher who meets certain minimum criteria such as career level. In this case, however, the quality of a match may still be tempered if the researcher does meet other preference criteria. Given how competitive the funding world is and the high numbers of candidates who may possess all the criteria for a match, the possibilities for alternate sponsors should be explored.

In any case, it must be possible to identify at least one prospective sponsor before proceeding to the next decision in the pathway. Similar to decisions at the preceding step, the decision here is binary: If at least one match exists, proceeding is reasonable; if no match exists, re-evaluating overall training goals and starting again is the best way to proceed for eventual success.

The Mentor Should Have Appreciable Expertise in All Areas of the Training Plan

One of the most important aspects of a career development plan is the selection of an appropriate mentor and the extent to which the mentor is dedicated to the researcher and the proposed work. As shown in Table 3.1, some funding opportunities require that a mentor be explicitly assigned to a program, and this assignment gains importance with any change in research direction of the trainee. However, even when the presence of a mentor is not a requirement, the experience offered by a senior person can be invaluable. Partnership with a mentor, even if informal, is always strongly advised.

A mentor should be chosen with several criteria in mind:

- Expertise in a specific area of a given field.
- National and potentially international recognition.
- Reputation as a teacher and mentor.
- Track record of trainees or mentored researchers.
- Number of other trainees during the proposed training period.
- Funding history, especially if the mentor has a track record of success with the prospective sponsor, either individually or with other researchers.

Given the growing complexity and interdisciplinary nature of research today, it can be desirable to have two mentors who bring complementary expertise to the program. Pairing a senior mentor to a junior mentor can also be a strong strategic move, especially when the junior mentor does not yet have a well-established research program or track record of training others. The number of mentors should be limited to two, however, because managing more than a pair, in terms of both logistics and expectations, can become unwieldy.

The role of any mentor should be well-defined in the context of the career development program so as to maximize the opportunities offered, and in the case of two mentors, to minimize overlap or redundancy. The relationship should be planned with respect to frequency and location of mentoring meetings, actual research obligations, and means of evaluating progress.

The queries at this point are:

1. Does the mentor or combination of mentors provide the scientific expertise necessary to supervise the training?
2. Does the mentor or combination of mentors have the time and interest in mentoring the prospective trainee?
3. Has the mentor or combination of mentors successfully mentored other trainees, as measured by career positions and funding obtained by previous trainees?

4. Does the mentor or combination of mentors have a track record of funding success that will help position the trainee to be competitive for funding?

If the answer to Queries 1 or 2 is no, it is advisable to rethink and reselect the mentor or combination of mentors, and then re-evaluate at this point in the pathway. If scientific expertise is lacking, or if the mentors already have too many other commitments, the program will not be likely to succeed. Evidence for or the perception of such circumstances would undoubtedly compromise the fundability of the program. If the answer to Queries 3 or 4 is no, it is advisable to select a co-mentor in the case in which only one was selected originally, or to reconfigure an original pair so as to correct for the deficiency. If an iteration at this point still does not yield a satisfactory result, it may be necessary to return to the level of the second decision, reformulate the actual career development goals of the program, and then re-evaluate again.

The Research Environment Must Be Able to Support the Career Development Goals of the Researcher

The research environment in the context of a career development program refers to both people and laboratory resources. A strong research environment—encompassing both these components—will almost always exist in parallel with a strong mentor, but certain criteria that distinguish outstanding environments versus acceptable environments can be defined. They are as follows:

- Open access to other researchers and clinicians within the institution and to those from outside who come as visitors.
- Quality of the other trainees.
- Availability of relevant courses, conferences, and seminars.
- Convenient and ample access to state-of-the-art equipment for the research project.
- Availability of appropriate subject pools.
- Travel budget.
- Office space, computers, and administrative support.
- Special resources.

Open Access to Other Researchers and Clinicians Within the Institution and to Those From Outside Who Come as Visitors. Openness in the research environment is enriching and enhances productivity. The degree to which an environment encourages openness and interactivity among its members should be carefully assessed when defining a career development program.

Quality of the Other Trainees. The presence of other good trainees in the research environment can be stimulating and supportive during career development. The common perspective from the point of view of career level makes other trainees valuable interlocuters and challenging scientific colleagues.

Courses, Conferences, and Seminars. The availability of relevant didactic courses, conferences, and seminars is key to a robust career development program, especially when the training is designed to round out previous training or bring about a career change. Participation should be encouraged, if not required, by the program sponsor and mentor(s), and should be well balanced against other training responsibilities. Because coursework provides the foundation for training, it is useful to complete it in the first phases of a training program (e.g., the first 12 to 18 months of a 3-year program). Attendance at and participation in conferences should also be an ongoing component of the training program; it has the effect of both exposing the new researcher to other research in the area, and of exposing the external environment to the new researcher. A robust research environment will be supportive of such activities.

Convenient and Ample Access to State-of-the-Art Equipment for the Research Project. Although a research environment may have the most modern equipment and tools, access to it by junior members of a laboratory, such as postdoctoral or career development trainees, may not be easy or sufficient. Take, for example, the case in which the training is focused on magnetoencephalographic (MEG) imaging, but the system is only available for 10 research hours per week for a laboratory of six researchers. Even assuming an equal distribution of the research time to all members of the laboratory, the question arises as to whether less than 2 hours of imaging per week will be sufficient to gain the desired experience and to fulfill goals outlined in a research plan (see discussion presented later in this chapter). In the case in which time on specialized equipment is allocated according to seniority, the consideration becomes even more acute. Therefore, when formulating a career development program, careful evaluation must be made of both the type of equipment available as well as access to it.

Availability of Appropriate Subject Pools. Different institutions draw different types of volunteers and patients. Therefore, if a program is focused on a specific clinical population, for example, that clinical population must be well represented in the environment. If not, or if in a given research environment a well-represented clinical population is already heavily studied and issues of access exist, it must be possible to identify a geographically reasonable alternative subject pool. If this is not possible, the suitability of the environment should be reconsidered because it will be unable to support the research component of the program.

Travel. Not all training programs provide a budget for travel to conferences, and most do not typically provide sufficient funds for travel to the many important meetings that occur per year. Therefore, the extent to which support is offered for travel from the sponsoring environment, be it in the form of actual funds or in the form of authorized leave, is another important consideration in the development of a career development plan.

Office Space, Computers, Administrative Support.
The availability of office space, computers and administrative support will depend on the extent to which the environment is well-funded and dedicated to its trainees. Easy access to these resources is an important factor in any training program.

Special Resources. Some research environments have invested in people to provide special resources to its researchers, such as experts in research program development, laboratory animal management, computer support, or visual arts. Such special resources will not be found in many training environments but can be invaluable during the formative stages of a career.

This decision is heavy with variables, but in reality, many outstanding research environments will be able to match most, if not all of them. When trade-offs need to be considered, they should be weighed carefully against both professional and personal goals.

The Research Project Must Explicitly Provide Hands-On Training in the Area Desired

The research project is a crucial component of the training program in that it provides the opportunity to translate new knowledge and theory into applied experience. It is essential, therefore, that the project be selected and designed to provide that hands-on training.

For example, a researcher may wish to acquire expertise in a new modality of imaging, such as functional MRI, when previous experience was limited to electroencephalography. The associated research should be based on a hypothesis-driven project that utilizes all aspects of that new modality, from data acquisition to data analysis. It is not inappropriate for the study to require a comparison of data acquired with the two modalities—in fact, this can provide valuable insight into the workings of the new method—but the primary focus must be on the new modality and the new information it brings to the problem area.

Similarly, if the training is for a shift to a new conceptual area (e.g., dysgraphia from previous experience in dysarthria) the project goal and hypotheses must be focused on that new area. Although this may seem obvious, there is a natural temptation to use tools known from an old trade for a new one; this is acceptable only when the tools from the previous trade are state-of-the-art and relevant to the new trade.

The two queries at this point, therefore, are:

1. Does the project create an experience in which the major potential of the new area is exploited?
2. Is the project design specifically matched to meet the goals of the overall career development program?

The answers to both these queries should be affirmative before proceeding to the next step. If not, the idea underlying the project should be iterated until these goals are achieved.

The Research Project Must Be Intrinsically Robust

A certain amount of scientific latitude exists in the conceptualization pathway for research projects that are embedded in career development programs as compared to the pathway for stand-alone projects (described in detail in chapter 2). Overall rigor, however, is an unwavering common criterion. The decisions for conceptualizing training research projects are as follows:

The Idea Should Be Grounded in Science. The salient feature of this decision is that the idea for the research should have a basis in science and not in intuition. There is latitude here in terms of project riskiness, however, provided that the project gives good exposure to the research field.

The Idea Must Have Merit. *Merit* is defined in terms of both need and impact, and takes into consideration all the parties in the research relationship (see Table 3.2). Briefly, need can be measured by the effect of a given problem as it exists today. Impact can be measured by the change that successful execution of the research will bring.

In the context of career development programs, the measure of need is as important as it is for self-standing research projects. Funding will not be available for a project that is carried out without any perceptible need for it. However, the question of impact is another matter. For training fellowships (i.e., training specifically for postdoctoral fellows, and to some extent for scholarships), the impact of the project can be incremental. The expectation for a major contribution is waived or limited. By contrast, for early career development awards for new faculty, the impact must be absolutely substantial with respect to the researcher's own career evolution and with respect to the world community.

The Project Must Have Realistic Deliverables. Deliverables form the hard core promise of the work on which success or failure are measured. Guidelines for developing sound deliverables

TABLE 3.2
Testing for the Merit of a Training Program

Need	Impact	Action: Postdoctoral Fellowship or Scholarship	Action: Faculty Career Development
High	High	Proceed to next decision.	Proceed to next decision.
Low	High	Proceed to next decision, but consider reformulation to reduce associated risk with low need.	Proceed to next decision, but consider reformulation to reduce associated risk with low need.
High	Low	Proceed to next decision.	Reconfigure project to increase the impact measure.
Low	Low	Proceed to next decision (risky).	Reconfigure project and reevaluate.
None	None	Abandon idea and try again.	Abandon idea and try again.

are discussed in chapter 2 and apply fully to research projects for career development programs. In addition to those guidelines, each deliverable for the research project in the career development program should be matched to a specific hands-on training component.

The Methods Must Be Sound. The key elements of the methods are the hypothesis or development objectives, rationale, procedures, data analysis, and experimental limitations, as discussed in chapter 2. Scientific rigor is a strict criterion that must be met for each of these elements.

The Expertise of the Research Team Must Match the Project Goals. Although the focus of the overall program is on the individual, it is uncommon for any one person, particularly a person in the stage of career formation or expansion, to be able to execute a research project single-handedly without the participation of or consultation with other researchers who have relevant expertise. Therefore, the project must either be designed so that complete autonomy is realistic, or so that the necessary (and willing) expertise is available. This includes, for example, technical, engineering, laboratory animal, medical, clinical, and statistical expertise. If it is not apparent that sufficient expertise exists to cover all the components of the project, then the project should be redesigned or other personnel recruited.

The Proper Resources Must Exist or Become Available.
Consistent with the need for appropriate expertise to carry out the project is the need for and access to the appropriate tools and space, as described previously. These must either exist or be borrowed, leased, or purchased. A project that does not have the necessary resources available to it cannot be successful and will not be fundable.

Proof of Concept.
Traditionally, preliminary results are gathered to demonstrate feasibility of a concept and to provide evidence that the researcher is qualified to do the work proposed. In training programs, at least some data for proof of feasibility are necessary; proof of competence is obviously less critical. The data should demonstrate that the concept is viable experimentally in terms of execution and that the outcome is likely to be meaningful. Feasibility is further strengthened when coupled with innovation, where the approach is unique and explores uncharted territory. When such data are accompanied by evidence of acceptability by peer review, either by the trainee, the mentor, or ideally by the trainee and mentor together, then proof of concept is even more profound.

The questions at this point, therefore, and the final questions for the conceptualization pathway of training programs are:

1. Do data exist to suggest that the concept is feasible?
2. Do the data support the timeframe laid out for the proposed work?
3. Do the data suggest that the concept is new and creative?
4. Do the data demonstrate that the research will be carried out competently given the support of the training experience and mentorship?

Undoubtedly, the strength of a proposal will be enhanced with affirmative answers to these four questions. However, because the research project is only a component of an overall training program, and proof of concept only a component of the project, this step is only a gatekeeper if preliminary data suggest that a project is not feasible at all.

SUMMARY

A summary of the critical common decisions in the conceptualization of individual career development programs—postdoctoral fellowships, scholarships, and faculty career development—are shown in Table 3.3. These same decisions apply to institutional

TABLE 3.3

**Summary of the Critical Decisions and Key Features
in Conceptualizing Training and Career Development Programs**

Critical Decisions	Key Features
Career independence	The program yields a researcher who is prepared to carry on the next steps in a career, and is qualified to train others and conduct research independently.
Training goals	There is a need and a place for a new researcher in the field.
Match with a sponsor	A sponsor with mutual interests and appropriate funding power can be identified to support the program.
Mentor expertise	A mentor or pair of mentors with appropriate expertise and sufficient time can be identified to advise the trainee during the course of the program.
Research environment	The research environment is robust in terms of quality and accessibility to people in the relevant field at all career levels, and in terms of educational opportunities, access to instrumentation, administrative support and special resources.
Research project	The research project—a single, but key component of the overall program—provides hands-on training and is intrinsically robust.

programs that are developed for the benefit of training multiple trainees at a time.

Funded career development programs provide superb opportunities to learn new skills or refine existing ones in a relatively independent and unstructured framework. Typically, these programs fit into the
early phase of a researcher's career and can be enjoyed prior to the
many responsibilities that accumulate with increasing seniority.

Chapter 4

Multicomponent Research Programs

Multicomponent research integrates activities across projects or research sites into a single program unified by common ideas and core resources. Multicomponent programs can generally be characterized by one of three distinct models: program projects, centers and consortia (Table 4.1). They share the common overriding theme that the strength of the integrated program exceeds the sum of the strengths of the individual parts.

PROGRAM PROJECTS, CENTERS, AND CONSORTIA

Program Projects

Program projects are comprised of individual research projects that are united for the purpose of achieving a common goal (Fig. 4.1). The projects may be linked to each other thematically (e.g., a given disease) or by application (e.g., a new method), and are further linked by common core resources such as subject pools, instrumentation and administration. The number of component research projects—typically three to five—and the number of cores—typically one to three—will vary according to overall program goals, set in careful balance with a prospective sponsor's interests and funding power. The components may be drawn from a single institution or from multiple institutions. Some sponsors, such as the Human Frontier Science Program (http://www.hfsp.org), actually require broad involvement of

47

TABLE 4.1
Purpose, Features, and Considerations of the Three
Major Types of Multicomponent Programs

	Program Projects	Research Centers	Consortia
Purpose	Enhance and accelerate multifaceted research dedicated to a common goal.	Conduct research dedicated to a common scientific goal: foster collaboration, provide access to specialized instrumentation and know-how, provide service, and engage in educational activities that extend outside the boundaries of the center.	Realize a program goal through the integrated efforts of sites with special expertise and through the statistical power afforded by pooled data.
Organizational structure	Single PI or co-PI partnership leads program effort; investigators are specialized to oversee individual research components; other personnel, collaborators, and consultants are appropriate as defined by the components and the cores.	PI or co-PI partnership leads scientific and administrative team.	Under the direction of a PI or co-PI partnership, central site sets the direction for the program and coordinates the activities of all the sites.

(Continues)

TABLE 4.1 (Continued)

	Program Projects	Research Centers	Consortia
Features	Accelerated rate of scientific progress; dynamic interaction among center participants; shared resources.	Internal productivity and external outreach.	Research opportunity that could not be realized without the concerted effort of laboratories that are otherwise unrelated.
Considerations	High cost of funding a large-scale program limits pool of prospective sponsors; complexities associated with managing and participating in a relatively large organization that is composed of individual research groups with individual priorities.	Same as for program project grants, plus the additional resources, organization, and budgetary load required to fulfill and maintain outreach goals successfully.	Authorship on publications is sometimes limited to investigators at the central site or to a smaller number of authors than those who carried out work; allowable budget allocation to each site may be less than the budget needed to carry out the work.

FIG. 4.1.   Schematic organization of program projects.

components from institutions in different countries to encourage international collaboration.

Management of program project grants is typically overseen by a single PI or PI/co-PI partnership. Each research component is led by its own PI. Each component is usually supported by its own research team, although it is not unusual for some team members to participate in multiple components.

The need for certain major core resources may also be met by instrumentation or construction programs (Fig. 4.2). These programs are characterized by the same model as program project grants, in which the acquisition of instrumentation, new space, or renovated space is justified by the needs of multiple researchers or research units. Grants formulated specifically for such core resources as op-

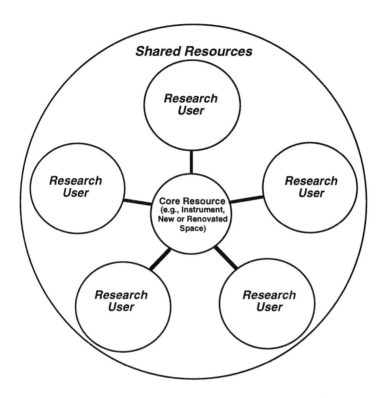

FIG. 4.2.   Schematic organization of research programs surrounding instrumentation or construction.

posed to core research, however, do not necessarily require collaboration among the resource beneficiaries.

Centers

Research centers embody program project goals as well as core outreach goals that include collaboration and service in research, education and training, and communication and information dissemination (Fig. 4.3). The goals of research centers, therefore, extend well outside their own walls—whether virtual or real—into the broad academic, corporate, and lay communities. To reflect this outreach feature, the structure of a research center may be viewed roughly as an inversion of the structure for program projects. The component research projects and associated resources form the nucleus, with the

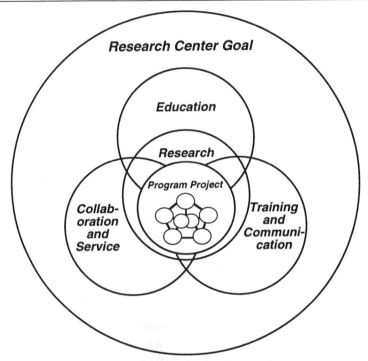

FIG. 4.3.   Schematic organization of research centers.

additional cores—the primary conduits to the outside world—residing peripherally.

Centers are typically directed by a single PI or PI/co-PI partnership. They are joined by co-investigators who have individual responsibility for the direction of the component research projects. The responsibilities for the core goals of the center are shared by all the investigators.

Consortia, Coalitions, and Cooperative Programs

Consortia, coalitions, and cooperative programs are formed from research sites brought together for the purpose of carrying out work according to a common protocol. One site serves as a coordinating site, and the others may either be self-selected or selected by the central site during program formulation. The sponsor may also select sites based on the evaluation of proposals submitted by interested parties. The work may be complementary from site to site, as in the hypothetical case of a consortium in which each site uses a different modality to provide psychological work-ups of women with schizophrenia. In this example, the consortium is designed to capitalize on the expertise offered by institutionally and potentially geographically dissociated research sites. Alternatively, the work may be cumulative, as in the case of clinical trials in which each site precisely follows a common protocol. Here, the ultimate goal is to gather more data into a larger data set than could be achieved by any single site.

This type of multicomponent program is characterized by the leadership of the coordinating site, and coordination and cooperation of the independent participating sites (Fig. 4.4). Furthermore,

FIG. 4.4.   Schematic organization of consortia, coalitions, and cooperative programs.

unlike program projects and centers for which regular interaction among participants is crucial, consortia members typically communicate about the program formally during planned meetings on a fixed schedule throughout the life of the program.

CONCEPTUALIZING MULTICOMPONENT PROGRAMS

The common decisions in the conceptualization pathway for multicomponent programs are shown in Fig. 4.5. The pathway for evaluating the competitiveness of multicomponent programs implicitly includes the pathway for evaluating single-component project-based research, and adds unique decisions that have to do with the links between the individual research components. The extra steps ensure that the program is cohesive, that the program deliverables are robust, and that the core resources support the program goal.

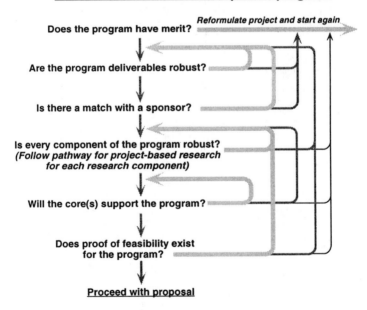

FIG. 4.5.   Conceptualization pathway for multicomponent research programs.

The Overall Program Must Have Merit

In consideration of the merit of a large-scale program, the need and impact of the whole must exceed the need and impact of the component projects executed individually. This measurable benefit is afforded by the interactions among the participating groups, the research that is stimulated and enabled by the common theme or unifying hypothesis, and overall programmatic momentum.

The merit of the program must also justify the relatively high one-time funding commitment that a sponsor must make compared to the commitment to single projects that are not necessarily time-locked. However, a multicomponent program may also save a sponsor funding dollars by centralizing expensive resources such as instrumentation. Moreover, over the long-term, a good multicomponent program will return far greater results per dollar in a shorter amount of time than a sequence of projects that are dedicated to the same problem area but are otherwise dissociated.

The query at this first point, therefore, tests for the merit of the program as a whole. It queries whether the complexities and costs of a multicomponent program are significantly offset by the benefits that will be realized through cooperative research, collaboration, data volume, and shared resources. If the answer to these considerations is affirmative, then it is appropriate to proceed to the next decision. If not, the program goals should be refined or reoriented, and then reevaluated.

The Overall Program Deliverables Must Be Robust

Program deliverables are generally broader than the deliverables of the component projects and, just as for projects, they may be development-driven or hypothesis-driven. A program may be driven, for example, by the development of a comprehensive neurologic examination for the substance abuser, in which the deliverables for the component projects culminate in discipline-specific or modality-specific screening tests. By contrast, a program may also be driven by a unifying hypothesis that, for example, predicts the fundamental mechanism for a disease process in the nervous system, and in which the project components are each dedicated to elucidating the mechanism from different points of view. Additional program deliverables, especially for research centers, may include expanded collaborative activity with outside laboratories, new courses or seminars, and training of students who, in the absence of a program, may not otherwise be trained.

Despite the broad nature of the program deliverables, they must still be as realistic and rigorous on a temporal and budgetary basis as project-based deliverables. Moreover, the program deliverables must embody all the component projects and be feasible given the program cores. Robustness of program deliverables, therefore, is measured by the ability of a program to deliver promised results as a function of several variables:

- The goals of the component parts.
- The appropriateness of the core components.
- The ability of an infrastructure to bring results together in a timely and meaningful way.

If this criterion for robustness is not met, then the program deliverables should be reconfigured, or the program reevaluated, before proceeding to the next decision.

A Good Match With a Sponsor Must Exist

Finding a sponsor may be one of the most difficult tasks to accomplish during the conceptualization and development of a multicomponent program. The quality of the match is measured by:

- The interest of a prospective sponsor in the overall program.
- The suitability of each component part to the interests of the sponsor.
- The economic reality of a large-scale program.

Because annual budgets can exceed $500,000, the pool of prospective sponsors is limited. Therefore, with the idea for a meritorious program and strong program deliverables in hand, it is essential to contact prospective sponsors early in the conceptualization process and assess the strength of the match and prospects for a funding relationship. At least one prospective sponsor should be identified before proceeding to the next decision. If it does not appear that sponsorship will be a reality, then naturally it will be more fruitful to reevaluate and reorient the program deliverables, and possibly even review program merit, than to continue further along the pathway.

The Program Must Be Composed of Strong Components

Research. Each research project component of a multicomponent program should be developed following the conceptualization pathway for project-based research, described in chapter 2 and illustrated in Fig. 2.1. Each research project must, therefore:

- Be grounded in science.
- Have merit.
- Be grounded in a compelling overall goal.
- Be well matched to a sponsor.
- Have realistic deliverables.
- Be sound experimentally.
- Be supported by an appropriate research team.
- Have the necessary resources.
- Be supported by proof of concept.
- Be personally desirable.

In addition to the project-centric considerations, the relationship to the overall program goal and to the other program components should be carefully developed throughout the conceptualization process.

Education. Educational components of multicomponent programs may have both professional and lay aspects. The component may include formal training of students, fellows, and visiting scholars, as well as opportunities for informal training for the nonspecialized public through courses and seminars. In conceptualizing the program, the number of personnel or allocated personnel effort should be correlated directly to training responsibilities.

Collaboration and Service. Collaboration with and service to outside laboratories can be significant components of multicomponent programs. In addition to promoting scientific progress, they allow for access to specialized resources such as expensive instrumentation and know-how. When formulating the plans for a multicomponent program in which collaboration and service are fundamental components, plans for managing them organizationally must be carefully formulated and milestones for success well-articulated.

Communication and Information Dissemination. A successful multicomponent program will deliver significant results consistently over time. Dissemination of results to the professional community through presentation at professional meetings and publication in the literature is a natural outcome, as is the dissemination of new technology in the case of research centers. Dissemination may be for actual technology that outside laboratories can acquire from the program and utilize, or updates about advancements in electronic or hard copy form. When developing the program, ample resources should be allocated for the communication component, as well as for providing follow-up support when the activity involves dissemination of new technology to new users.

The queries at this point are, as follows:

1. Does each individual research project component pass the test for competitiveness as defined by the conceptualization pathway for project-based research?
2. Do the training, collaboration and service, and dissemination of information components meet the requirements for cohesiveness, organizational rigor, realistic resources and a realistic budget?

If the answer to the first query is negative, then the relevant research projects should be reworked at the relevant steps until the criterion is met. Similarly, if the answer to the second query is negative, then the relevant component should be reworked until organizational, resource, and budgetary requirements are met.

The Core(s) Must Be Able to Support
the Program

The core components of a multicomponent program are, on the one hand, the supporting features of a program, and on the other hand, the unifying ones. An administrative core is required for any multicomponent program. Additional cores may be for instrumentation, laboratory space, shared observation or conference rooms (possibly built or renovated), or specialized biostatistical expertise. Taken together, the cores should encompass all the common needs of the individual components and be accessible within an organizational framework in which the components can interact and can leverage on the accomplishments of one another.

The queries at this point are as follow:

1. Is each identified core relevant to all the components of the program?
2. Are all the necessary cores identified?

If a core does not serve all the components, it is important to consider whether it should be eliminated or allocated to the individual components to which it is relevant. In parallel, it is important to revisit the individual components because it is possible that with some refinement, the identified cores become essential to each one.

With respect to the second question, and regardless of the complexity of a program, all core resources needed for the delivery of program goals must be clearly identified. This is essentially the same query as for project-based resources, except on a considerably larger scale. The number of cores should typically not exceed three or four, and the criterion must be met before proceeding to the last decision in the pathway.

The Program Must Be Feasible

Feasibility of a multicomponent program is measured on the basis of both science and organization.

Scientific Feasibility. The determination of scientific feasibility considers:

- Evidence for the promise and innovation of the research proposed.
- Evidence that the anticipated results of the individual projects will support the overall scientific goals of the program.

These criteria reiterate the need for the components to be unified thematically and by a common hypothesis or development goal.

Organizational Feasibility.   Organizational feasibility is measured in both history and future planning. The history measure queries whether the researchers have a track record of successful collaboration. This may be evidenced, for example, by previous collaborative work among members of the program team, or by the pre-existence of a smaller, successful group that can be regarded as a model for the program.

The question of future planning is concerned with how well the program is organized:

- Scientifically, in terms of goals and personnel.
- Administratively, in terms of leadership and support.
- Pragmatically, in terms of daily communication, access to core resources, and means of prioritizing complex program aspects and potential conflicts.
- Objectively, in terms of advisory structures.

The history query also considers the promise of success and the uniqueness of the program given similar programs that preceded it or that would exist contemporaneously with the one proposed.

Given the overall investment in a multicomponent program required from both the proposing group and a prospective sponsor, each of these criteria must be met unequivocally. Iterations at the levels of the fourth and fifth decisions may be necessary until all the criteria are met.

SUMMARY

The pure scientific desirability of a multicomponent program should be weighed against the internal organizational load on the participating research teams and against the eventual external cost to a prospective sponsor. The justification for a large-scale program should also take into consideration the need for core components, the concomitant funding needed to support the cores, and the cost associated with rapid progress and extended scientific interaction. However, when the justification for a multicomponent program is strong, the opportunities for great productivity and impact in a concentrated period of time are great.

A summary of the critical decisions and the key features of the programs are shown in Table 4.2.

TABLE 4.2

Critical Decisions and Key Features of Multicomponent Programs

Critical Decisions	*Key Features*
Program merit	The overall need for a cohesive program and the anticipated impact surpass the combined need and impact of the component parts.
Strong program deliverables	The deliverables that drive the program represent the unified goals and anticipated results of each of the components.
Match with a sponsor	A sponsor can be identified whose interests and priorities match those of the overall program and the individual components, and whose funding power is sufficient to support a program of the magnitude projected.
Strong components	Each component individually meets the rigorous criteria set for project-based research and the requirements for training, service and communication success.
Strong supporting cores	Core activity and resources fully support the program and unify the individual components.
Program feasibility	Evidence exists for the scientific, innovative, and organizational promise of the program.

Chapter 5

Small Business Innovation Research and Small Business Technology Transfer Programs

OVERVIEW OF THE PROGRAMS

The Small Business Innovation Research (SBIR) and Small Business Technology Transfer Research (STTR) programs in the United States provide the researcher-entrepreneur in a small business with the opportunity to conduct research that will culminate in a commercial product. The program was created under the Small Business Innovation Development Act of 1982, and reauthorized in 1992 to encourage small businesses to pursue technology for the benefit of stimulating technological innovation, utilizing small business concerns to meet federal R&D needs, fostering and encouraging participation by minority and disadvantaged persons, and increasing private sector commercialization of innovation (http://www.doe.gov).

The program requires federal agencies with an extramural budget of over $100 million to reserve a percentage of it for the SBIR/STTR programs. The percentage has grown from an initial 0.2% in fiscal year (FY) 1983 to a maximum of 2.5% in FY 1997 (http://www.doe.gov). In 1998, roughly 10 federal agencies have SBIR programs, with several thousand active NIH-sponsored SBIRs and about 300 STTRs in various phases, each responsive to a need that is of mutual interest to the sponsor and the small business. SBIRs and STTRs may support any type of commercial product, such as devices, videos, educational material, and software.

TABLE 5.1
Three Phases of SBIR and STTR Programs

Phase	Goal	Restrictions
Phase I	Establish the technical merit and feasibility of the proposed innovation.	Not designed for testing feasibility of product production.
Phase II	Complete full-scale development and testing.	Only available to Phase I awardees.
Phase III	Commercialize product.	Only available after Phase II.*
		Requires nonfederal funding.

Around the time that this book went to press, NSF implemented an SBIR Phase IIb that provides for an additional 12 months of support to companies that have at least $200,000 committed to a product from the private sector.

The programs are divided into three phases (Table 5.1). The first two are supported by the federal sponsor. The first phase is for proof of feasibility (i.e., theoretical or experimental investigation of a product idea). The second phase is for product refinement, implementation, and full-scale testing. Third phase commercialization must be made with independent funding.

For the purpose of the SBIR and STTR programs, small businesses are defined as for-profit, independently owned organizations with 500 or fewer employees. No preference exists between the start-up comprised of a handful of employees and a large organization with significant longevity, per se, but socially and economically disadvantaged concerns and women-owned businesses are particularly encouraged to apply.

The fundamental distinction between the SBIR and STTR mechanisms is involvement of a third party: for SBIRs, the involvement of a research partner is limited to a subcontractual relationship of less than 33%; STTRs are specifically designed to foster technology transfer through fully cooperative R&D relations between small businesses and research institutions. The differences are summarized in Table 5.2. In 1998, the award rate for SBIRs and STTRs is approximately 25% to 30%; 12% to 35% for Phase I proposals; and up to 50% for Phase II SBIRs (70% for the few existing Phase II STTRs).

TABLE 5.2

Key Features of SBIRs and STTRs

	SBIR	STTR
Award	Phase I: $70,000 to $100,000	Phase I: $100,000
	Phase II: $200,000 to $850,000	Phase II: $500,000 to $600,000
Award Duration*	Phase I: 6 months to 1 year	Phase I: 1 year
	Phase II: 2 years	Phase II: 2 years
Principal Investigator	Must be employed by the company more than half of the time during the award.	Minimum 10% effort on project.
Involvement of Subcontractors & Consultants	May not exceed 33% in Phase I, and 50% in Phase II.	Subcontract to a partnering institution is required at a level of at least 30%.

Adapted from NIH Web Page (http://www.nih.gov)
*Exceptions to prolong the award duration may be granted with proper justification.

FEDERAL SBIR AND STTR SPONSORS

Table 5.3 shows examples of the federal SBIR and STTR sponsors, their respective missions, and some example program areas. Many of the Department of Defense programs emphasize "dual-purpose" projects in which the research is expected to serve both military as well as civilian needs.

It is conceivable that a single innovation may require sponsorship by serial Phase I awards, each of which underwrites a different research component. Ultimately, the Phase I grants converge on a single Phase II. When this is the case, it is important to ensure that the various Phase I components are complementary and nonoverlapping, and equally important to plan early (i.e., before the first Phase I is submitted), with the prospective program manager.

TABLE 5.3

Representative SBIR and STTR Programs

Sponsor	Type of Award	Mission	Example Program Areas
National Institutes of Health	SBIR STTR	Bioscience research with disease-related goals, including etiology, diagnosis and treatment of physical and mental disease, abnormality and malfunction in human beings and animals.	Dementia, alcoholism, imaging, assistive and rehabilitation-related technology, biological models, reduction of the use of vertebrate animals in research.
National Science Foundation	SBIR	Cutting edge, high-quality scientific, engineering, or science/engineering education research.	Biological sciences; social, behavioral, and economic sciences; education and human resources.
Department of Defense	SBIR STTR	U.S. Military and economic strength.	Biological sciences.
Office of Naval Research	SBIR	Advancement of science and technology serving the needs of the Navy.	Cognitive and neural sciences.
Air Force Office of Scientific Research	SBIR	Timely transition of affordable and integrated technologies to serve the needs of the Air Force.	Cognitive neuroscience.

(Continues)

TABLE 5.3 (Continued)

Sponsor	Type of Award	Mission	Example Program Areas
Food and Drug Administration	SBIR STTR	Protection of public health by ensuring that food, medical devices, and biological devices are safe and effective.	Radiation monitoring; medical devices; safety and efficacy of drugs.
Centers for Disease Control	SBIR STTR	Disease prevention and control, environmental health, health promotion, and health education.	Disease prevention; occupational safety; nonoccupational environmental factors.
National Center for Environmental Health	SBIR	Promotion of health and quality of life by preventing or controlling disease, injury, and disability related to the interaction between people and the environment outside the workplace.	Hearing loss in children; environmental hazards; drinking practices in women of reproductive age.
National Center for Infectious Disease	SBIR	Improvement of the identification, investigation, diagnosis, prevention, and control of infectious diseases.	Drug susceptibilities; bacterial diseases; vaccine immunogenicity.
National Center for Injury Prevention and Control	SBIR	Maintenance and improvement of health by preventing premature death and disability, and by reducing human suffering and medical costs.	Interventions for intentional and nonintentional injury; acute care; assistive devices; trauma or spinal cord injury.

(Continues)

TABLE 5.3 (Continued)

Sponsor	Type of Award	Mission	Example Program Areas
National Immunization Program	SBIR	In collaboration with the World Health Organization and the Center for Disease Control, coordination of immunization programs to control disease.	Community assistance.
National Institute for Occupational Safety and Health	SBIR	Development and implementation of occupational safety and health standards.	Hazards in the workplace; protective equipment.
Department of Transportation	SBIR	Maintenance and advancement of a transportation system that meets the vital interests of the nation and enhances quality of life.	Performance assessment; screening.
Department of Energy	SBIR	Fostering of energy systems that can be sustained environmentally and economically, and that support U.S. Leadership in science and technology.	Health and environment; computation and technology.
Department of Education	SBIR	Promotion of literacy, lifelong learning, and independence of persons with disabilities.	Individual learning and workplace performance; adult literacy; minorities in scientific, technical, teaching, and health career fields.

Certain agencies, such as the Department of Energy, have implemented a new mechanism to expedite movement of an innovation from its early phase to a more complete and well-funded one. Known as *fast-track*, the mechanism allows both Phase I and Phase II proposals to be submitted simultaneously. The advantages and disadvantages of pursuing the fast-track opportunity are summarized in Table 5.4.

TABLE 5.4

**Advantages and Disadvantages of the Fast-Track
SBIR and STTR Opportunity**

Advantages	*Disadvantages*
No gap between Phase I and Phase II funding.	Stringent milestones must be set at the time of Phase I; the plans for meeting those milestones and for managing any unexpected events must be dealt with rigorously in the discussion of the Phase II plan.
Requires more detailed long-term planning than for Phase I alone.	If the Phase II plan is unsatisfactory, the entire proposal will be unsuccessful, even if Phase I alone is meritorious and fundable.
Brings an early commitment from a nonfederal partner to the innovation.	A detailed product development plan of up to five pages is required.

CONCEPTUALIZING SMALL BUSINESS
RESEARCH GRANTS

Phase I SBIRs

Figure 5.1 shows the decisions in the conceptualization pathway for Phase I SBIRs. This pathway also forms the foundation for the Phase I STTRs (Fig. 5.2) and the Phase II SBIR and STTR programs (Fig. 5.3).

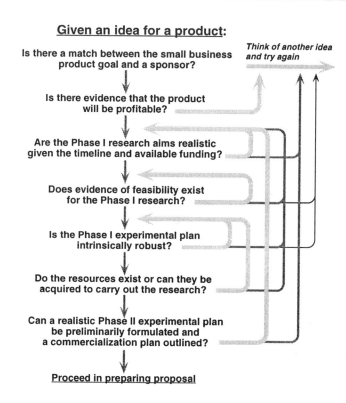

Given an idea for a product:

Is there a match between the small business product goal and a sponsor?

Think of another idea and try again

Is there evidence that the product will be profitable?

Are the Phase I research aims realistic given the timeline and available funding?

Does evidence of feasibility exist for the Phase I research?

Is the Phase I experimental plan intrinsically robust?

Do the resources exist or can they be acquired to carry out the research?

Can a realistic Phase II experimental plan be preliminarily formulated and a commercialization plan outlined?

Proceed in preparing proposal

FIG. 5.1. Conceptualization pathway for Phase I SBIRs.

A Match Must Exist Between the Product Goal of the Small Business and the Need of a Sponsor

SBIR proposals must be specifically responsive to a published need, priority area, or interest of a sponsor. The match should encompass the approach to the product development research and the end-product itself. For example, the U.S. Air Force is likely to be a good prospective sponsor of a product for rapid testing of cognitive fitness for pilots. By contrast, a video-based, self-help nutritional health series may be best matched with one of the health-related sponsors from NIH, such as National Institute of Mental Health or National Institute of Aging, with the Food and Drug Administration, or with the Department of Education.

When a match exists fortuitously with more than one sponsor, then the decision as to which sponsor to pursue becomes a pragmatic one. The pragmatic factors include the following:

- Award amount.
- Award duration.
- Proposal deadlines.
- Duration of the review cycle.
- Requirement for commitment to the product from a third party.
- Funding paylines.
- A commitment to bridge funding between Phase I and Phase II awards, a particularly important consideration for start-ups whose income and operating budget are dependent on the award.

There is a single query that must be met at this point, therefore:

1. Does an explicit match with a sponsor exist for the product idea?

This query takes into consideration both the type of technology to be developed and the application. If the answer to this query cannot meet both conditions, then the product idea should be reformulated; it may retain the technology modality but require a new application, or vice versa. However, the match should be complete before proceeding.

There Must Be Evidence That the Product Will Be Profitable

For the researcher who does not have a background in business administration, profitability of a product may be predicted by the following few factors:

- Target market and demand.
- Projected cost of the product.
- Anticipated longevity of the product before it becomes obsolete or has to be revised.

Target Market and Demand. The target market represents the people who will be interested in purchasing a product, such as a certain age or professional group, hospitals, academic institutions and private sector organizations. The target market is further defined by the geographical appropriateness and desirability of a product. For example, an educational nursing software application geared for rural communities may, on the surface, appear to have a smaller market-place than a product that is not designed specifically for a subpopulation of the profession. However, when a real need exists for such a product, even if need the exists only in the rural community, then the product has a market.

The next question is whether the product can be developed cost-effectively. That is, will it be affordable to the target population when it is ready to be commercialized, and will it have a wide enough distribution so as to be profitable for the organization developing it? These factors should be carefully assessed when formulating the product plan.

The issue of target and demand coincides with the question of scientific merit (i.e., need and impact) because these define the potential market. Without both, the profitability of a product will be difficult to realize. Table 5.5 summarizes these criteria and trade-offs.

Projected Cost of the Product. The projected cost of the product at the time that a Phase I SBIR is being developed should be derived from the manpower needed to produce it, the cost of materials, the cost of manufacturing, marketing and distribution, and the pro-

TABLE 5.5
Testing the Merit of a Product Idea

Need	Impact	Action
High	High	Proceed to next decision.
Low	High	Proceed to next decision, provided that the market is large enough to justify the costs of the investment in the innovation.
High	Low	Proceed to next decision, but Phase I should include tests of acceptability to determine how the low impact will affect the success of the innovation.
Low or none	Low or none	Reconfigure the concept for the innovation so that at least need or impact can be projected to be high, or develop another idea.

jected sales. The value of the product standing on its own compared to the value of competing products, should also be factored into its projected price.

Anticipated Longevity of the Product.   The longevity of the product as conceived in the present, and the potential cost of updating it in the future, are the final rudimentary factors in projecting product cost for an SBIR proposal. Because only projections can be made at the time of early development, the risks can be minimized by careful analysis of the success or failure of similar products.

The queries at this point, therefore, are as follows:

1. Will the final product cross a threshold of demand, based on principles of need and impact, to justify the research and development investment?
2. Will the product be affordable in the target market?
3. Will the product have sufficient longevity to justify the initial research and development investment?

The first two queries are gatekeepers in the pathway. If a product is not likely to be profitable because the demand does not exist, or if the product is likely to be too costly to be successful in the target market, then the product should be reconceptualized. Although SBIR sponsors are committed to promoting technological innovation, it is unlikely they will invest in technology that does not have a reasonable chance of success and that, in turn, will not serve their own mission.

Product longevity is not necessarily a gatekeeping factor. For example, as in the case of software, it is possible that the need for and impact of a product will be time-limited, but that in a given timeframe, it will be highly successful. In the conceptualization process, therefore, longevity should be evaluated in the context of both long-term as well as short-term return.

Phase I SBIRs Must Have Realistic Deliverables

The deliverables for the Phase I SBIR should be milestones that represent significant scientific advancements related to a product idea (i.e., basic research), as well as progress toward its development. The deliverables may be either development-driven, hypothesis-driven, or both, as discussed in chapter 2, and the promised results must be deliverable within the 6-month or 1-year Phase I funding timeframe. Because SBIRs are highly technology-based, Phase I deliverables will commonly include engineering milestones, such as the fabrication of a prototype device or software programming, which are followed by testing of the prototype in an experimental setting. Phase I deliverables should also include consideration of informal feedback, and time permitting, analysis of formal (i.e., hypothesis-driven and statistically-driven) prototype acceptability tests. Phase I SBIR deliverables may not, however, include marketing research or literature searches or reviews because these tasks should have been completed as part of the proposal development process.

The queries are as follows:

1. Does the set of deliverables represent a logical first step in producing a technological innovation?
2. Are the deliverables logically linked in a conceptual way to one another? For example, in the case of software program development, are the different application platforms evaluated before programming is begun?
3. Are the deliverables logically linked in a pragmatic way to one another? For example, is the chronology of deliverables reasonable and efficient?
4. Will each deliverable itself yield a meaningful result or significant step toward the accomplishment of the project goal?

With affirmative answers to each of these queries, both the proposal and first phase of product evolution can be successful. Reconceptualization of one or some of the deliverables is recommended if any one of the queries yields a negative result. If repeated iteration of the deliverables still does not yield a positive result, the process should be reinitiated at the level of the first decision.

The Phase I Research Plan Must Be Sound

Conceptualization of the research plan for the Phase I SBIR follows all the critical steps of designing experiments for project-based research, as described in chapter 2. The research plan must conform

entirely to the deliverables specified, and for each deliverable, there
should be:

- A study or set of studies driven by a development objective or hypothesis.
- A rationale.
- A rational procedure or set of procedures.
- A means of data analysis.
- A means of dealing with unexpected results.
- An anticipated significance.

Once an initial research plan is drafted, it should be reviewed objectively for its overall cohesiveness and its potential to meet the requirements for Phase I success. Before proceeding to the next step in the pathway, the answers to the following questions should all be affirmative:

1. Is there a study with a driving hypothesis or development objective for each deliverable?
2. Is the rationale for each study well-justified?
3. Are the experimental procedures scientifically rigorous and constructed in a way that they can be tested to yield meaningful results?
4. Can the limitations of the steps in the research plan be addressed and are the means of dealing with unexpected findings and obstacles defined?

There is little flexibility at this point; therefore, the research plan should be iterated until each of these criteria is met. If necessary, redesign the deliverables and reevaluate at the level of the third decision.

Small Businesses Must Have the Resources or Access to the Resources to Conduct the Work

According to SBIR guidelines, the small business must either serve as the principal site for the work or control the research site. Therefore, if the resources do not exist to carry out the work, then they must become available either through the SBIR award or through another sponsor. If the resources do not exist or cannot be obtained, then the research plan or project deliverables should be redefined so that the project goals match project resources.

The Phase I Plan Must Show That a Scientifically and Financially Feasible Phase II Can Be Formulated

It is not necessary in Phase I to enter into an elaborate discussion of the Phase II plan. It is necessary, however, to provide evidence of long-term planning, and evidence that the long-term plan will culminate in further realistically executable research. For example, a device that is tested in a phantom model in Phase I may require full scale testing in an animal model in Phase II. It is important to discuss broadly the next steps for the Phase II, as well as needed resources. If, in developing this section, significant obstacles become apparent, reevaluation of the project should begin at the first relevant point where the obstacle can be identified.

There Must Be Evidence That a Phase III Plan Can Be Executed

As in the previous step, an overview of the critical steps needed to realize success of the innovation are required. In Phase I, it is sufficient to name prospective Phase II partners; in Phase II, the list should be narrowed to a single partner and accompanied by a letter of commitment to the commercialization phase. In both Phase I and Phase II proposals, a general marketing plan should be presented to provide evidence that the innovation will successfully reach the intended marketplace. If such a preliminary commercialization plan cannot reasonably be conceived, reevaluation of the project as high as the second decision may be necessary.

Phase I STTRs

The conceptualization pathway for STTRs (Fig. 5.2) is generally the same as for SBIRs, but takes into consideration the existence of an academic partner for the short-term and potentially for the long term. Therefore, the third decision in the Phase I STTR pathway explicitly

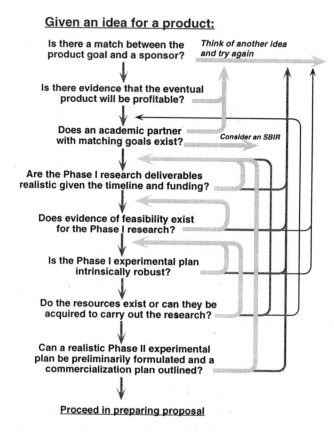

Given an idea for a product:

FIG. 5.2. Conceptualization pathway for Phase I STTRs.

considers whether an academic partner with matching goals exists. If a suitable partner cannot be identified, or if an agreeable partnership cannot be developed, the options are to consider an SBIR or, alternatively, to reevaluate the product plan entirely.

The sixth and seventh decisions also distinguish STTRs from SBIRs in that they query whether the involvement and responsibilities of each partner are clearly defined and appropriate and whether the necessary resources to carry out the work plan are available at each site. Should this not be the case, the project plan should be iterated at the nearest points upstream of decisions about the experimental plan or resources, until the necessary criteria for proceeding are met.

The gatekeeping criterion for STTRs is that a significant partnership (i.e., one that exceeds the 33% allowed by SBIRs) brings unique advantage to the product innovation process. The expected benefit of the Phase I work to each partner, and plans for the continuing relationship of the partners through the Phase II and Phase III work should be developed and articulated as early as possible during the conceptualization process.

Phase II SBIRs and STTRs

The decisions in the Phase II SBIR and STTR pathways (Fig. 5.3) are similar to the decisions for Phase Is, except where the decision is either not relevant to the Phase II, or must be updated.

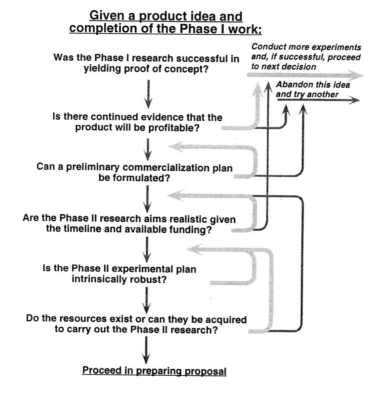

FIG. 5.3. Conceptualization pathway for Phase II SBIRs and STTRs.

At the first decision for Phase IIs, the match with a sponsor is assumed and it is replaced with a decision that considers the successes and failures of the Phase I work. The Phase II proposal is predicated on the success of the Phase I research (provided that the submissions are serial and not fast-tracked, as previously discussed). Therefore, the concept of *success* in this context must be defined. Assuming that (a) the goal of Phase I is to support the exploration of a new idea, (b) development goals are based on knowledge and past experience, and (c) testing is hypothesis-driven, it is conceivable that not all aspects of the Phase I plan will yield expected results. The expectation that unpredicted findings will emerge, in fact, is built into the research plan, as described in chapters 2 and 6. Nevertheless, in consideration of these assumptions, success is defined by the entire profile of the innovation given both the positive and negative results of Phase I work. For example, Phase I research may have revealed that a software program for second-language learning will have high acceptability, but only if it runs on a faster platform than originally planned. With the backing of strong acceptability results, and the real possibility for a faster program, the Phase II plan may be realistic. By contrast, if Phase I research failed to demonstrate that a prototype system will ever be operational, acceptable, or desirable, then Phase II is not likely to be successful.

When Phase I yields equivocal data or data that are difficult to translate into a convincing Phase II, a brief period of focused, interim research that is self-funded or funded by another source (possibly even by another Phase I) may be necessary to complete an experimental profile that will lead to success.

At the level of the third decision for commercialization, the Phase II pathway considers the prospective Phase III plan. Significant evidence for commercialization support and commitment in the form of a marketing plan or intended partnership is expected at the time that the Phase II is submitted.

The principles for proceeding at Decisions 4, 5, and 6 (i.e., mapping project deliverables onto a budget and timeline, experimental plan, and resources) are the same as for Phase I proposals, except that the project timeline is now considerably longer and the budget substantially larger.

SUMMARY

Small business innovation research and technology transfer research are exciting opportunities to link basic science directly with application. The critical decisions common to them are summarized in Table 5.6.

The pre-award process is demanding, and the post-award timeline is structured to be fast-paced. For very small businesses such as start-ups, the risks of relying solely on SBIR/STTR funding to develop a product and meet an operating budget are relatively high; for businesses that are small but well-established, the risks are relatively less significant. For both, however, the opportunity to become partners with a federal sponsor whose basic requirement is benefit to society and who takes no portion of the profit made possible by its initial investment is extraordinary.

TABLE 5.6
Critical Decision Nodes and Key Features
of SBIR and STTR Research

Critical Decisions	*Key Features*
Match with a sponsor	Priority area and budget are met by at least one sponsor.
Product profitability	Need for and eventual impact of a product will translate into a return on the initial investment.
Deliverables	The deliverables realistically map on to an allowable timeline and budget.
Proof of concept	Data exist to demonstrate project feasibility and innovation.
Experimental plan	The scientific approach is rigorous and a plan exists for handling unexpected results.
Resources	The resources exist within the small business and with an outside partnering organization to carry out the work proposed.
Future development	Realistic plans for product development beyond Phase I and into Phase II and Phase III can be envisioned.

Chapter 6

Translating Research Ideas Into Written Proposals: Scientific Sections

SETTING THE TONE FOR THE SCIENTIFIC SECTIONS AND CONFIGURING A ROAD MAP

The scientific sections of a proposal, whether for a single component or complex program, must be rigorous and detailed. Proposals are generally built around the scientific sections that reflect the critical steps in the conceptualization process: deliverables, rationale, significance, preliminary results, and experimental plans. This chapter focuses on the strategies for writing clear, powerful, and mutually supporting scientific sections. Many of these strategies can also be adopted for oral presentation of scientific proposals and site visits.

THE PROPOSAL SUPERSTRUCTURE

Sponsor Instructions

The single dominant guideline in proposal preparation is the need to follow precisely a sponsor's instructions. Each proposal must be customized to meet a prospective sponsor's requirements, even if it is for the same project as originally submitted elsewhere. This can sometimes be painful, admittedly, especially when it appears that the instructions will not lead to the most logically constructed or cogent proposal. However, the goal is to submit a proposal exactly the way a sponsor wants to see it, from the organization of the proposal itself to the manner in which it is bound. In the worst case, a proposal may be returned unreviewed for failure to follow a specified format; in the less severe case (albeit still undesirable), an unfavorable disposition towards a proposal by a sponsor can be created by virtue of a researcher's apparent inability or unwillingness to follow a requested format. Always be sure, therefore, that instructions in hand are complete and up to date. Also note that when responding to an RFA or RFP, any specific instructions in the solicitation prevail over instructions that correspond to a related standing program.

Presentation and Tone

Consistent with the need to respect the sponsor's instructions is the need to submit a document that respects the reviewers. The formatting should be consistent, the text should be free of spelling and typographical errors, and the language should be easy to understand. Errors and inconsistencies render a proposal difficult to review and, moreover, they create a sense of carelessness and poor planning that tends to raise questions about whether the research will be performed with the same poor quality control as the proposal itself.

It is also important to set an overall tone of confidence at the beginning of the proposal that endures throughout the text. This tone will emerge from a combination of clean presentation, clearly articulated ideas, and consistency of the major proposal themes throughout the proposal. Commitment and confidence should always be balanced against overconfidence, since the latter can have the undesirable effect of distancing rather than attracting a reviewer. For example, an effective statement such as: *"Upon successful completion of this work, we will have revealed mechanisms in the evolution of cystic fibrosis that will lead to the development of new treatments for patient management and care"* can be contrasted to a statement that is too weak: *"If successful, this work may help to impact the lives of many patients afflicted by cystic fibrosis"* or to one that is too strong: *"Our success will be reflected by a significant change in health care for all patients with cystic fibrosis."*

Whenever possible, commitment and confidence should be substantiated by previous relevant publications and other relevant evidence, such as a track record of successful collaboration among the investigators.

The tone of a proposal should also reflect the quality of a match with a sponsor. In an investigator-initiated proposal, the quality of the match can be implicit throughout the proposal by consistency of the central idea. When a proposal is submitted in response to an announced opportunity, the quality of the match should be made explicit by the use of wording that is consistent with the wording in the announcement.

Legends and Tables

Legends or captions are needed for every figure, table and image in a proposal. Groups of figures, tables, and images should be numbered separately across groups (e.g., Table 1 ..., Figure 1 ...) but consecutively within groups (e.g., Table 1, Table 2). They should contain a succinct title and an explanation of the importance of the data. The legends should be offset by formatting (e.g., change of font size, italics, margins), and should be consistent throughout the text. For example:

> *Table 1: Analysis of reaction times to auditory stimuli. Reaction time data are shown for the control (untreated) and attention deficit disorder (ADD) groups in the quiet and auditory-masked (noise distraction) conditions. Analyses reveal a significant difference between the two groups for the masked condition only.*

(Given a figure with four images)
> *Figure 7: Progression of stroke volume over time. Progression of stroke volume over four time points in a representative case of a 72-year-old male: (a) immediately after onset, (b) 3 months after onset, (c) 6 months after onset, and (d) 18 months after onset. The MRI images clearly depict an increased volume at the acute timepoint (compare Images a and b) that stabilizes over time (Images b, c, d).*

When allowed, key figures, illustrations, or images should be reproduced in an appendix because some sponsors may keep originally submitted copies of a proposal for their files and distribute photocopies of potentially lesser resolution to reviewers. However, in most cases, the figures must still appear in the text in order to avoid using appendices as a way of bypassing page limitations.

References

A single format should be adopted for the references. The format should be used consistently throughout the text and in the reference section, and can be based on a format used in any major journal in the field.

Tense

The recommended tenses for the scientific sections of a proposal appear in Table 6.1.

TABLE 6.1
Tenses for Scientific Sections of a Proposal

Section	Tense
Deliverables	Future, as in: *"We will identify ..."* *"We will characterize ..."*
Background, rationale, significance	Present, as in: *"There are 200,000 new patients diagnosed with breast cancer every year ..."* Past, as in: *"The work of others has shown ..."*
Prior work, preliminary results	Past for actions; present for results as in: *"We observed that bipolar shifts are exacerbated by stress ..."* *"We showed that programmed cell death is accelerated in the presence of ..."*
Experimental methods	Future, as in: *"We will measure" ... "We will test ..."*
Product market and profitability	Future, as in: *"We estimate that with the more than 200,000 new breast cancer survivors in the United States each year,, affordable computer-based instruction for self-relaxation and self-hypnosis will yield a high return on the initial investment in R&D and production."*

(Continues)

TABLE 6.1 (Continued)

Section	Tense
Career statement	Past, present, future, as in: *"I received my doctoral degree at Whimer University in Massachusetts, where my research was focused on the effect of maternal cocaine use during pregnancy on postnatal development ... Through the training program proposed here, I will extend my knowledge base to disorders and drug pattern usage in adolescents, in particular as they are correlated to maternal drug use. Upon completing this fellowship, my goal is to find a university position where I will be able to teach, continue to conduct research, and make contributions in this field."*
Justification for a multicomponent program	Present and future, as in: *"This program brings together the expertise of nationally respected laboratories in the neurosciences, enabling wide-scale, multidisciplinary collaboration on multiple sclerosis. The common goals, opportunities for daily interaction, joint supervision of students, and jointly sponsored conferences promise to yield advancements in fundamental knowledge and patient care that will far exceed the sum of the progam's parts."*
History of a small business (SBIRs/STTRs)	Past, present, future, as in: *"Cestine Inc. was established in 1992 as a woman-owned small business focused on the needs of battered women. Cestine's mission is threefold: (1) to serve as a national referral service for therapy, refuge, and education; (2) to conduct research on the long-term effects of domestic violence; and (3) to produce self-help material in the form of books and videos. Cestine's products will respond to the vital need for affordable and easy-to-access material that addresses problems, opportunities, and solutions in a frank and realistic way."*

Further guidelines and recommendations for communicating effectively in writing are presented at the end of this chapter.

DELIVERABLES AND PERFORMANCE GOALS

The Scientific Road Map

The deliverables section, typically about one page long, forms the foundation for the proposal and should encapsulate all the key elements. It should provide the context for the research, delineate the aims, provide an overview of the experimental approach, and make a statement about the anticipated impact of the work in the short term and long term. The basic pattern, therefore, looks like this:

(where x = subject matter)

1. x exists and is defined as …
2. However, x currently has these limitations
3. Our work will extend x by …
4. This will enable … This will have the following effect …

The deliverables section should be written before starting any other section to provide the organizational structure—the road map—for each section to follow. In essence, each subsequent section then becomes an expanded discussion of the themes presented in this one.

Setting Context

The context for the proposed work should be created in the lead paragraph with a few sentences (one to five sentences) about the overall goal, merit, current state-of-the-art, limitations of the state-of-the-art, and how the proposed work will address the limitations to meet the need. The first sentence alone is key, as illustrated in the following example:

(Effective)
*Functional imaging of the brain with magnetic resonance tech-
nology is a new approach to understanding the neural substrates
of human language behavior.*

(Too broad)
*The field of psychology has experienced much change over the
past century, especially with the evolution of technological approaches to brain function.*

As a guiding principle, the first paragraph is a place for very specific statements that focus entirely on the work proposed. For example:

*Functional imaging of the brain with magnetic resonance tech-
nology (fMRI) is a new approach to understanding the fundamental processes underlying human language behavior.
Whereas other imaging modalities such as PET and EEG have
yielded substantial knowledge about both the anatomical and
functional substrates of language processing, they have been
limited by their invasiveness (PET) and spatial resolution
(EEG). fMRI is a recently developed approach that is unencum-
bered by these limitations. However, its widespread clinical application for surgical planning is hampered by the need for
specialized imaging hardware. Our goal is to advance the technical potential of fMRI fully so that it can be utilized readily in
both basic research as well as in the clinical environment. To this
end, our specific aims are: ...*

Statement of Deliverables

A specific description of the deliverables should follow the lead
paragraph. Each deliverable should be described as a tangible result
anticipated from an experiment or set of experiments. Deliverables
should contain a predicate and an object, and should not be written
as phrases or questions. For example: "*... To this end, our specific
aims are: Aim 1: To determine the accuracy of the proposed new
psychometric technique for identifying reading disorders*" com-

pared to: *"Aim 1: What is the accuracy of the new psychometric test?"* where the question cannot specify a deliverable, and compared to: *"Aim 2: New test for reading disorders"* where short phrases are uninviting and ineffective.

In addition, because deliverables are the core promise or contract for work, they should be stated in a manner that conveys the delivery of an end-product. This is driven by the choice of words used to convey the message. For example: *"To determine ..." "To identify ..." "To characterize ..." "To reveal ..." "To elucidate ..."* are far more powerful phrases than: *"To understand ..." "To study ..." "To examine ...,"* which explain what the researcher will pursue but not what the research will accomplish.

The statement of each deliverable should be accompanied by a hypothesis or goal, as appropriate. As discussed in chapter 2, hypotheses must be formulated using constructs that are testable statistically, and they should be written so that they directly support the deliverables. A deliverable with an accompanying hypothesis that only vaguely relates to it will be intrinsically weak. Similarly, a hypothesis that includes an *and/or* clause is formally implausible, and should be reformulated and rewritten. For example:

We hypothesize that interferon and/or acyclovir will mediate the progression of cognitive decline in HIV as measured by performance accuracy on tests of working memory and/or the loss of sensorimotor acuity as measured by tests of accuracy and speed in finger tapping.

This four-in-one hypothesis would be more correctly written as four separate hypotheses:

We hypothesize that:

Interferon and acyclovir, alone or in combination, will mediate the progression of:
(1) the cognitive decline in patients' HIV+ as measured by performance accuracy on tests of working memory,
(2) the loss of sensorimotor acuity in patients HIV+ as measured by tests of accuarcy and speed on finger tapping.

The deliverable and hypothesis are then further developed by a brief statement about the experimental approach to the problem. For example:

Aim 1. Interferon will mediate the progression of the cognitive decline in HIV as measured by performance accuracy on tests of working memory. We will test this hypothesis in 40 HIV+ men and women performing the PASAT. Twenty volunteers will be treated with interferon and 20 will receive a placebo in double-blinded fashion. The data will be acquired at two time points, within 3 months of first presentation of cognitive symptoms and 18 months thereafter, and tested using conventional multivariate statistics.

If a deliverable reflects a goal-driven task rather than a hypothesis-driven experiment, then a measurable endpoint or set of endpoints should be specified. For example, if an aim is to deliver a new brain biopsy device that is not at an experimentally testable stage yet, then the endpoint for determining when the design is ready to be converted into a prototype should be clear. This may be tied to the point at which the design meets all criteria or a predetermined composite of criteria specified, for example, by a set of experiments based on phantom models.

When appropriate, it may be desirable to cluster deliverables into superordinate categories such as technical development (usually goal-driven or a combination of goal-driven tasks and hypothesis-driven experiments) or clinical testing (almost always hypothesis-driven), especially if the categories are coincident with actual phases of work.

Statement of Anticipated Outcome

The deliverables section should conclude with a final paragraph of one to three sentences that states the anticipated direct outcome of the work in terms of the aggregate of all the deliverables, the future work it will lead to, and the long-term impact on the world community. For example:

Following successful completion of this work, we will have demonstrated the effects of interferon and acyclovir on cognitive and sensorimotor functions in early HIV+. We will conduct studies

in the future, under follow-on funding, to further refine dose pa-
rameters and maximize the benefits of the therapy for patient
groups in both early and late HIV stages.

Summary

To summarize this section on deliverables, the first paragraph presents the significance of the proposed work in terms of need, the context in terms of the state-of-the-art and its limitations, and the overall goal of the work in terms of how it addresses current limitations and will advance the state-of-the-art. The first paragraph also sets up the forthcoming list of specific deliverables by including a statement about the experimental plan. A final paragraph brings closure to the section by reference to research that may be conducted beyond the period of the proposed work, and returns to the issue of the significance of the work in terms of impact.

Developing the deliverables section using this framework is an effective way of reassuring reviewers that each step of the research plan has been worked out. Each deliverable is justified, and there is a logical connection between them.

Some research program developers view that a first context-setting paragraph and a final forward-looking paragraph are excessive, and that an itemization of the deliverables is sufficient to fulfill the requirements of this section. However, it is not sufficient. The goal is to present your research plan in such a careful and well thoughtout manner that the reviewer will have no questions about your purpose. If this section is written well, it will give the reviewer confidence that the plan is worth considering carefully. As in scientific papers or abstracts, results are not simply listed, they are presented within a context that provides the rationale to the work on the one hand, and an interpretation of their meaning on the other. A similar framework to the one described here is a key feature of a successful deliverables section of a scientific proposal.

BACKGROUND AND RATIONALE

The background section should be dedicated to a review of the literature, and almost exclusively to work performed by others than the proposing team. It is useful to think of the background section as an opportunity to point out to the reviewer both the accomplishments in a given field and its limitations. A discussion of previous accomplishments speaks to the history and context of the need, and the limitations point out that the need is not yet fulfilled. The objective, therefore, is to set up the reader to anticipate and appreciate presentation of the proposing team's preliminary results that address the stated limitations.

A structured literature review that relies on subsections is one of the most effective ways of guiding a reviewer through the text. First, it forces an organization that ensures that individual topics are clearly introduced, fully developed, and then brought to closure. Second, by virtue of the visual clarity afforded by subsection headings, the structure provides a surface representation to the reviewers of the topics the researchers chose to cover. The order of the subsections should coincide with the order of the deliverables; each subsection should begin with an introduction or overview, and conclude with a summary of the main points of that subsection.

Subsections should be numbered and formatted meticulously for easy reading. For example:

B.1   *Overview: Medical Relevance*
B.2   *Pharmacotherapeutic Approaches to the Treatment*
         of Depression
B.2.1 Serotonin Inhibitors
B.2.2 *Dopamine Inhibitors*
B.3   *Nonpharmacologic Approach to the Treatment*
         of Depression
B.4   *Summary*

Subheadings should always be referential, that is, they should provide enough independent information so that a reviewer can scan them, and, without reading the text, have a good overview about the messages of the section and the information therein. Nonreferential subheadings such as *Other Issues, Additional Information,* and *Miscellaneous Items* should be avoided.

The final summary of the entire section should succinctly reiterate the main points raised in the constituent subsections and, ideally, draw them together in a conclusion that highlights the need for the work being proposed.

SIGNIFICANCE

Some sponsors require a combined background and significance section, while others require a separate discussion for each. When combined, the significance should be discussed in one of the first subsections to address the issue of need (as in *Overview: Medical Relevance,* in the previous example) and in the summary paragraph to address the issue of impact. However, when the format dictates separate sections, the significance in terms of need should be addressed in the background section, and the significance in terms of impact should be reserved for the separate significance section. The stated impact should express a measurable outcome, for example, an actual change in people's lives, or a significant contribution to a relevant field. As discussed in previous chapters, if a case cannot be made for significance, the idea should be reformulated because it is not likely to be fundable.

Overall, a stand-alone significance section is likely to be briefer than the background section. A structured approach with subsections is recommended, nervertheless, because it will most effectively communicate the significance of the research to the reviewers.

PRELIMINARY RESULTS, PRIOR WORK

This section in a new proposal (progress reports are discussed in chapter 10) allows the researcher to deliver evidence that the proposed work is feasible and innovative, that the results are compelling, and that the researcher and the team have the expertise to accomplish the proposed work. It is important to provide substantial detail in this section, even if it repeats information provided elsewhere, such as in the methods section. It is also essential to supply the best illustrations, tables, and graphs in this section to reinforce the strength of the data and the overall credibility of the proposed work. References to and discussions about the work of researchers not associated with the proposal should be kept to an absolute minimum in this section; such discussions should have been taken care of in the background section because they may otherwise detract from the work being proposed.

As before, a heavily structured approach that relies on subsections with referential subheadings is essential. The section should be introduced with a lead paragraph that explains the general history or context of the prior work and the overall logic to the preliminary experiments that were conducted in specific support of the work proposed. For example:

C.1 Overview
During the past 8 months, we have developed a new prototype device for testing auditory comprehension and have conducted four experiments to test its performance characteristics. The technical developments leading up to the prototype and the promising results of the performance tests are described here.

Then, each next subsection should be devoted to a deliverable with the accompanying hypotheses, experiment, results, and, finally, conclusions that link the results to the current proposal. A final paragraph should close the section by summarizing the overall approach to the work and the overall findings. In doing so, the significance in terms of impact of the work to date, the work that remains to be done, and the promise of the work should be highlighted. For example:

C.4 Summary
The preliminary data suggest that, with further refinement, the new system has the potential to revolutionize current methods for testing auditory comprehension and identifying speech and language disorders earlier than ever before.

There are several simple guidelines to follow in selecting which results are presented in this section, especially if page limitations are restrictive:

1.   Present only the most relevant and robust results. Omit nebulous or equivocal data.
2.   If an appendix is permitted, create one with publications that contain relevant results. Refer to the results and summarize them, but do not reproduce them at length in the body of the section unless they

are critical to the proposal. Do not rely on the reviewer to look up your prior work in the literature.

3. Articulate that the results presented are representative of a greater body of data, if appropriate. Specify how they have been chosen, and briefly summarize other relevant data. However, never be so obtuse as to say: *"Among many results ..."* without addressing, at least briefly, what the other results were.

One of the greatest challenges in the development of funded research is achieving a balance between the amount of preliminary data needed to show feasibility and virtual completion of the work. Conceptually, this balance may be achieved with about 10% to 20% of the work in the form of preliminary data. This is a very general estimate, however, that must be refined for each situation.

EXPERIMENTAL DESIGN AND METHODS

The methods section is the core of the proposal and should map on to the deliverables section. The section should be prepared with absolute clarity and rigor, and every component of the section should be proactive with respect to the work proposed. It is important to prepare a methods plan that carefully follows a timeline and a budget that are consistent and realistic. This plan must allow the rationale for selected approaches and analyses to be readily appreciated. However, this section is not the place for background, references to other work, or retrospective discussion.

As for the previous sections, the methods section will be easiest to appreciate if crafted using the familiar framework: overview of the section, the component subsections, and then a summary encapsulating the main features.

Overview

In a short lead paragraph, provide an overview of the proposed methods. Reiterate the overall goal of the research, state the number of deliverables and phases of work or experiments that are planned, and state the projected duration of the work. For example:

The overall goal of our work is to improve the detection and treatment of bipolar mood disorders. Toward this end, we propose three studies that will further elucidate the basic pathophysiology of the disease. The requested funding period is 4 years, as shown in the timetable below.

Timeline and Text of the Methods

The components of the timeline should map directly onto the major experimental subsections of the methods section. The timeline should be visually simple and easy to understand. The headings should match, as closely as possible, the subheadings used in the text. The sample timeline presented in Table 6.2 would be a good match for text that is developed according to the following outline:

D.2 Technical Development
D.2.1   Prototype Design
D.2.2   Testing of Parameters in a Phantom
D.2.3   Refinement of Parameters and Validation
D.3 In Vivo Testing
D.3.1   Performance Reliability
D.3.1.1   Hypothesis
D.3.1.2   Methods
D.3.1.3   Results
D.3.1.4   Limitations of the Experiment
D.3.2   Acceptance Testing
D.3.2.1   Hypothesis
D.3.2.2   Methods
D.3.2.3   Results
D.3.2.4   Limitations of the Experiment
D.3.3   Reproducibility
D.3.3.1   Hypothesis
D.3.3.2   Methods
D.3.3.3   Results
D.3.3.4   Limitations of the Experiment
D.4 Summary

TABLE 6.2

Sample Timeline

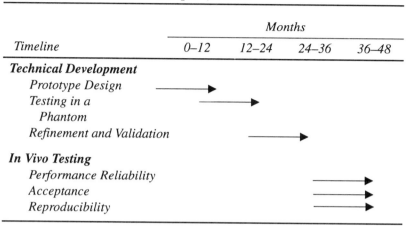

Timeline	Months			
	0–12	*12–24*	*24–36*	*36–48*
Technical Development				
Prototype Design				
Testing in a Phantom				
Refinement and Validation				
In Vivo Testing				
Performance Reliability				
Acceptance				
Reproducibility				

For all sections, correct usage of the terminology for procedures is essential, as in the example: *"We will compare measurements of performance accuracy using the new test and the conventional test"* compared to the less accurate statement: *"The new technique will be compared with measurements from the conventional technique"* where the sentence implies that a technique will be compared to measurements.

Limitations of the Work and Obstacles

Every methods section should contain a discussion of the possible limitations of the proposed work, as well as a discussion of possible unexpected results or obstacles and how those will be treated. This can be done on a deliverable-by-deliverable basis, or at the end of the presentation of all the methods, depending on where the discussion will be most logical and easy to appreciate. The extent of the discussion may be a brief representation of alternate methodological approaches, or a more fully elaborated alternate methods section. The length and depth of the discussion should be driven by the severity of the anticipated obstacle to the evolution of the work.

Summary of the Methods Section

This brief, one-paragraph subsection should restate the expected short-term outcome of the work, the overall rationale to the approach, and the overall expected impact of the work on the field and the global community. This final paragraph will complete the framework for this section, and should bring closure to the entire body of the major scientific sections.

OTHER MAJOR SECTIONS
DEPENDENT ON THE TYPE OF PROPOSAL

Whereas deliverables, background, significance, prior work, and methods are sections common to most proposal formats, other sections may be equally important, depending on the type of proposal. For example, the description of the unifying features of a consortium for a multicomponent program is a critical feature of the written proposal; the description of a mentor and a career plan is key to a proposal for training funds; the description of market potential, ideas about eventual product commercialization and company history are key to small business proposals. In all these sections, subsections defined by good subheadings will be most effective in ensuring that the necessary points are made. Further guidelines for these sections are provided here.

Special Sections for Multicomponent Programs

Proposals for multicomponent programs typically require a discussion of the unifying scientific goals of the program and the pragmatic and organizational plans governing the program.

Unifying Goal

This section must create a compelling argument for the goals of the multicomponent program and for its component parts. The section should begin with a statement about the goals of the program, the need for the program, and the anticipated short-term impact. It must address how each component of the program is individually essential to the success of the whole. This point should be made clear with respect to both suitability and intrinsic strength of each component.

The organizational plan for collaboration and communication among components must also be addressed in this section (discussed in more detail below). The plans can draw on any prior track record of collaboration by the investigators, such as co-authored publications or co-sponsored supervision of students, courses, and seminars.

Finally, the section should conclude with projections for the program in terms of its expected longevity and value.

Administratives and Organizational Structure

Any program that has multiple components will require time and effort to administer. The amount and quality of that time will be dictated by how well a structure is set up to manage multiple investigators, organizations, and geographical sites. Therefore, this section must clearly describe plans for program oversight, decision-making and prioritization procedures, and administrative support.

An organizational chart is recommended for illustrating the personnel structure, as well as the structure of local and external advisory boards, as appropriate. The accompanying text should describe the responsibilities of each major division of the organization, and define the means and frequency with which the divisions and members will meet to report on progress. For the reviewer, it is also reassuring to learn that an advisory group has been assembled not only for post-award oversight, but also for the pre-award proposal activity. If minutes are available from a planning meeting that included the advisory board, for example, a summary of the minutes may be included in the body of the proposal or the actual minutes may be included in an appendix as evidence of this activity.

Special Sections for Training Grants

The most common supplementary sections in a career development proposal are overall training plan, selection of a mentor, career plan, and training environment.

Training Plan.
For many sponsors, the quality of the training experience overall is more important than the research itself. Therefore, the overall training plan and the section that describes it should be developed thoughtfully and thoroughly. Using ample subsections, the section should include the following:

- A description of the rationale for the program.
- A schedule according to which each of the components of the training plan will be carried out.
- Milestones according to which performance will be evaluated.

Mentor. The following factors will be important to a reviewer when considering the suitability and strength of a mentor:

- Relevant professional history.
- Current interests.
- Past students and their career accomplishments.
- Current students.

These factors will be considered in terms of both the richness of the research environment and the workload of the prospective mentor. Each of these issues should be made into a subsection for ease of reading; alternatively, tables can effectively communicate the information. Table 6.3 is a sample of a well-constructed training history table.

TABLE 6.3

Training History

Past Trainees (Past 3 years, 27 since 1982)	Current Position
Jan Jones, PhD	Assistant professor, University of Oakdell, Department of Neurological Sciences
Grugh McVeigh, PhD	Associate professor, Wealington University, Department of Neurological Sciences
Ivette Laffand, PhD	Associate professor, Vennter University, Department of Education
Simpson Pesaf, MD	Associate professor, Gull State University, Department of Hearing and Speech Sciences
Current Trainees	Sponsor
Wilder Jazet, MD	NIH training fellow
Greta Olde, MD	NSF Young Investigator

Career Plan. Post-award career goals should be consistent with the training interests of a sponsor. For example, if a sponsor's goal is to train researchers for academia, then teaching and research should be clearly articulated career goals. By contrast, if a sponsor's goal is to provide research training to broaden the skills of clinicians, then a career that combines clinical research with clinical practice would meet the criterion for the match.

To this end, the description of the career goals should be written in a chronology that begins with the earliest relevant training experiences and mentors. The goals of each experience should be described, as well as accomplishments such as results and publications. The discussion should then describe what was learned broadly in each experience, and how that knowledge, combined with the direction and teaching of the mentor, impacted the decision to pursue the currently proposed career path.

The section should end with well-articulated goals for contributions to the field, justification of the need for additional researchers in that field, and the way in which the goals fit into a long-term career plan.

Training Environment. The written proposal should convey to the reviewer that the appropriate environment exists for the training proposed. As described in chapter 3, criteria for *appropriateness of the training environment* include the following:

- Access to and requirements for participation in courses, conferences, and seminars.
- Access to scientists other than the mentor.
- Access to and quality of other trainees.
- Availability of and access to the necessary materials to carry out the research proposed.
- Availability of office space, computers, libraries, and special resources.

The training environment will have a profound impact on the training plan. Therefore, each criterion should be addressed explicitly, with a discussion that includes both merits and limitations. A structured approach with clearly identifiable subsections is recommended here again.

Special Sections for SBIRs and STTRs

The special sections for the small business proposals include company history, anticipated marketability of a product, and a commercialization plan. As discussed before, a structured approach with subsections that follows a chronology of past accomplishments, present goals, and future projections will be most effective in communicating this information to reviewers.

SUMMARY

Good writing will not save a poor idea, but poor writing and poor presentation will jeopardize even the best one. Clarity, rigor, and confidence, as outlined in Table 6.4, are the key features to the written product. Therefore,

- Know your audience.
- Understand the review criteria, if available.
- Follow the sponsor's instructions precisely and write for that audience specifically.
- Double check the proposal for language, formatting, and miscellaneous errors. Enlist a colleague to provide an objective review and edit the document. This is especially important if submitting a proposal in a language other than your mother tongue.
- Set and maintain a tone of confidence and significance.
- Carefully lay out ideas so that they are presented in a consistent and linear way within and across sections of the proposal.
- Be proactive in the proposal by providing a clear path to the reader about rationale, approach, expectations, and limitations of the research.

TABLE 6.4
General Recommendations for Communicating Effectively in Writing

Do	*Do Not*
Use active writing, as in: *"We will test ..."* *"We predict ..."*	Use the passive form, as in: *"It is desired ..."* *"It is planned ..."* *"It is anticipated ..."* *"It is hoped ..."* *"It was shown that ..."*
Use parallel writing (i.e., if the text introduces a series of concepts that will be discussed in detail later, the order of that discussion should follow the order in which the concepts were first addressed).	Change the order of concepts from the order in which concepts are first introduced. Change the number of themes across sections.
Use abbreviations for terms that are long or difficult to read, especially if they are used repeatedly. Terms should always be defined meaningfully at their first appearance; their abbreviations should be used consistently after that point.	Use abbreviations cavalierly, since a proposal that is replete with abbreviations can become cumbersome.
Write with confidence, as in: *"Our results will impact ..."*	Hedge by using phrases such as: *"should yield ..."* *"might result in ..."* *"could lead to ..."*
Be detailed and precise.	Be wrong scientifically.
Strive for clarity and thoroughness. For example, if a finding is unexpected, explain why, as in: *"This result is surprising because ..."*	Use extra words and interjections that do not provide information, as in: *"Interestingly ..."* *"Curiously ..."*

(Continues)

TABLE 6.4 (Continued)

Do	Do Not
If a list of examples or references would be too long to provide completely,select a few good ones from it, as in: *"This result is consistent with findings reported by other laboratories (e.g., Karpar, 1984; Yurz, 1993; Zerfez et al., 1996)."*	Use *etc.* as in: *"This result is consistent with findings reported by other laboratories (Karper, 1984, etc.)"* Your *etc.* may be very different from your reader's.
Be succinct, as in: *"We will perform ..."* *"The results will demonstrate ..."* or even more boldly, if true, *"The results will show, for the first time ..."*	Use extra words that unnecessarily temper a message, as in: *"We <u>plan to</u> carry out experiments ..."* *"We <u>intend to</u> perform ..."* *"The results will <u>help to</u> elucidate ..."*
Write formally, as in: *"Unlike animal experiments, therefore ..."*	Be quip or use colloquialisms, as in: *"So, unlike animal experiements ..."* *"This research will determine if people who have experienced stress in their workplace have an ax to grind with their employers."*
Make a point if it is significant.	Couch issues as a matter of interest, as in: "Incidentally,this is also relevant to other models of ..." Use formatting (i.e., highlighting by <u>underlining</u>, **boldfacing**,or printing words or phrases in all CAPITAL letters) rather than content to make your point.

(Continues)

Table 6.4 (Continued)

Do	*Do Not*
Use positive words, as in: *"We will continue to search for ..."*	Use words with negative connotations, as in *"We were disappointed ..."*
Format for easy reading.	Use fonts that are too small or difficult to read.

Chapter 7

Translating Research Ideas Into Written Proposals: Administrative Sections

The accuracy of administrative details and the presentation of the entire document are important attributes of any research proposal. The quality of the presentation of the administrative sections can be viewed as a direct reflection of the quality with which a grant will ultimately be administered, and attention to detail in the preparation stage suggests attention to detail in execution. Therefore, it is important to ensure that all required administrative information is provided, that the budget is calculated correctly, biographical sketches are complete, statements about other sources of funding are up to date, and issues related to the use of animal and human models are addressed. This can be a cumbersome part of the proposal preparation, especially in light of the significant work required to develop an outstanding scientific plan; however, for the recipients of the proposal, administrative perfection is essential.

PROPOSAL TITLES

Proposal titles should be easy to understand, refer to, and remember. Some sponsors place restrictions on the number of allowable characters for titles, but even without this external constraint, a good title will not exceed roughly 60 characters. Because project titles are often searched by interested parties, ideally they should be simple and concise, and contain the approach or method and the problem area, as in the following examples:

"Functional Neuroimaging of Short Term Memory"
"Evoked Potential Studies of Reflex in Cerebral Palsy"
"Longitudinal Study of Depression in Breast Cancer Survivors"

or even just the problem area, as in:

"Hemispheric Lateralization in Autism"
"Mood Changes in Schizophrenia"

Titles for training proposals should focus on the research area, and should be structured in the same way as for projects. In general, there is no need to use *"Training program in ... "*.

However, in the case of a multicomponent program, the title should indicate the type of program because that will define its organizational structure and the problem area. For example:

"National Consortium on the Study of Post-traumatic Stress"
"Pacific Regional Center for the Development of Functional Neuroimaging Technology"

Titles for small business proposals follow the same rules, with the focus on the product to be developed and the target area:

"CD ROM-based Continuing Education in Psychiatry"
"Advanced Methods for Multichannel ERP Recording"

By comparison, wordy, excessive titles are less effective:
"Auditory versus Visual Memory: New Imaging Approaches to Dissociating Underlying Neural Mechanisms"

This may make a good manuscript title, but is too complex for the purposes of a proposal.

"A Unique Approach to the Development of Tests for Pain in Spinal Cord Injury Patients"

This latter example is relatively vacuous because it focuses on the development of tests (*Unique Approach to ...*) *rather than on the application of the tests themselves. It may be better written as "Nerve Fiber Tests for Pain in Spinal Cord Injury."*

Finally, because funding for grants and contracts is ultimately for research that has yet to be carried out, it is also not appropriate to use a title that is a conclusion, as in *"The Right Prefrontal Area as the Driver of Adaptive Self-Monitoring Behavior."*

Again, this may be an intriguing title for a manuscript or book, but its conclusive nature renders it unsuitable for a proposal title.

One last issue in formulating a title is that it should convey a priority match with a target sponsor. Consider, for example, *"Devices for MRI-Guided Therapy"* and *"MRI-Guided Therapy of Brain Cancer."* Although the first title may be the most forthright in that the research will focus on devices that could be applicable broadly to many aspects of therapy guided by magnetic resonance imaging, the second is far stronger by virtue of its focus on the clearly identifiable programmatic area *brain cancer.*

KEY WORDS

Certain sponsors require a list of key words, as in the case of federally funded small business proposals. Key words have the dual purpose of assisting program officers in making correct assignments for review and in maintaining databases of proposals received, awarded, and rejected. The selection and order of key words is a nontrivial matter, therefore, and carefully selected key words can be as beneficial as poor selections can be detrimental.

The principles for selecting key words are as follows:

1. The first two or three key words should address the overall theme of the proposal (e.g., learning disabilities, stroke).
2. The next key words should broadly specify the research problem area (e.g., dyslexia, aphasia).
3. The final key words should indicate the research approach (e.g., FDG PET, diffusion-weighted MRI).

Broad terms such as *imaging techniques* or *standardized tests* should not be used because they do not convey specific information.

COVER PAGES

Formats for cover pages to proposals are as diverse as the number of sponsors to whom proposals are submitted. Some are forms that must be filled in (e.g., NSF, NIH); others must be created free form. Regardless of the level of creativity required, meticulousness and accuracy are the prevailing considerations.

In the case of free-form cover pages, the title of the proposal, name of the PI and the co-PI, corresponding address, period of the proposal, and type of program to which it is responsive should be clearly stated. In some cases, the bottom line budget (total or per year) and key words should also be specified, and signatures of the PI and institutional official provided. Use the sponsor's instructions as your guideline, and make this front door to your proposal as inviting as possible.

ABSTRACTS

Abstracts provide the summary of the work proposed and, depending on a sponsor's requirements, will have to be suitable for review by peers (technical abstract) or by nonscientific persons (general abstract). The common objective, in either case, is to convey all key aspects of the proposal succinctly and convincingly. The distinguishing features are the language and technical detail that are used to convey the central message.

A structure that supports a strong technical abstract is as follows:

- Statement of the problem.
- Statement of the state of the art (i.e., the field to date).
- Summary of the overall objective of proposed research.
- List of specific aims.
- Anticipated short-term outcome of the project.
- Possible long-term impact of the project.

For example:

We propose to design a device for ablating small tumors within the central nervous system. While current technology allows for effective ablation of relatively large lesions, we will develop a probe will that transmit and focus energy with highly controlled heating to small (2mm) target tissue sites. We will initially evaluate two system designs in in vitro phantom tests, and utilize the best-performing design in subsequent studies. The variables for choosing the best design will include ease of probe use and control of the spread of thermal energy to nontarget areas. In the second phase of the work, we will develop a protocol for utilization of the probe in a rat model (n = 6), in which regions of the basal ganglia will be ablated. Ablated regions will be evaluated histologically to specify the primary site of ablation, volume of secondary spread to nontarget areas, and cell loss. Efficacy of the device and procedures will be analyzed again in consideration of ease of probe use and control of spread of heating. Upon successful completion of this work, we will have developed and tested a new means of ablating suspicious neural tissue that is more specific and less invasive than conventional procedures used today. Follow-up funding for a large animal study and subsequently human clinical trials will be the future steps in bringing this technology to the foreground of treatment of subcortical diseases.

This structure will be effective regardless of whether the abstract is limited to 250 words—in which case approximately one sentence per statement is needed, as in the example just shown—or for abstracts that may be as long as a full page, and which allow for slightly greater expansion of each major statement.

The structure for a general abstract is similar to that of a technical abstract, but the content should focus more on the significance of and rationale behind the research approach, rather than on the details of the methods themselves. The specific aims should be consolidated, and jargon and assumptions that the reader has knowledge about the scientific and technical motivations for the work should be avoided. Overall, this type of abstract can be viewed as a brief summary about why the work should be carried out and what it will deliver. Using the following structure,

- Significance of the problem.
- Statement of the state of the art.
- Statement of overall objective of proposed research.

- Summary of specific aims.
- Anticipated short-term outcome of the project.
- Possible long-term impact of the project.

An example of a general abstract follows:

The purpose of this work is to develop and test a new instrument that will make procedures for treating diseased tissue in the brain and spinal cord easier and safer than is now possible. The instrument will be designed to transmit powerful energy to very specific areas, with as little spread as possible to nontarget areas. Through tests in nonliving models, we will study the performance of two different designs. The accuracy and controllability of the better-performing design will then be tested in a small animal model. These results will be essential for future research which will be conducted using an optimized instrument design. Upon successful completion of the work proposed here, we will have developed and tested a new means of destroying potentially cancerous tissues in a way that is less costly and causes less discomfort than many brain and spine procedures today.

As a general rule, all abstracts should be designed to entice the reader to continue on for further detail.

EXECUTIVE SUMMARIES

Unlike an abstract that is expected to encapsulate the motivation and main objectives of a research proposal, the purpose of an executive summary is to convey all the main aspects of a proposal with enough detail so that its merits as well as limitations can be immediately appreciated. Executive summaries may also contain specific administrative information, such as the composition of the research team and the project timeline, that can be easily appreciated and evaluated.

Ideally, space for the executive summary will be unlimited, and can accommodate, under separate subheadings, an introduction, rationale, summary of the funding request and a summary of the vision for the work.

Introduction

The introduction of the executive summary serves two purposes: first, to state the overriding goal of the proposal, and second, to provide a definition of the criteria used to select the sponsor to whom the proposal is being sent. This is probably the only opportunity for explicitly stating why you believe the sponsor should partner with you on the proposed work.

For example,

Introduction
Our goal is to create a multidisciplinary center for clinical research in epilepsy at Williams James Hospital, the primary teaching hospital for Rhode Medical Center. We share the vision of the Longel Foundation that basic research is necessary to further elucidate the pathophysiology of epilepsy and that nonsurgical methods for treatment must be developed. We seek support from the Foundation, therefore, to achieve our goals.

Rationale

The rationale should provide clear statements about the need for the proposed work, how the need will be addressed by the work proposed, and the anticipated impact. It is important in this section—particularly when addressing the second point—to present how the work will benefit from the research team's prior history of success, as well as how it might build on or complement other research that is funded and ongoing in parallel with the work proposed. For example:

Rationale
Advances in the neurological sciences and medicine over the past two decades have transformed the care of epileptic patients. Whereas high dosages of pharmacologic agents, often accompanied by the need for repeated open surgery, were the norm in the past, today we are able to intervene and manage epilepsy relatively less invasively and with similar efficacy. We believe that continued advances in neurobiology, neurosurgery, and imag-

ing technology hold great promise for bringing significant changes to these patients, but if the achievements in the individual disciplines are not well-integrated, the field will remain fractured and major improvements elusive. We will assemble a group of outstanding neuroscientists, physicians, and engineers at our Medical Center to achieve the needed integration of disciplines and convergence of goals, and to revolutionize the field for the direct benefit of the patient. Through this effort, we will rapidly transfer new advances from the bench to the bedside, train students and fellows to become future leaders in the field, and effectively disseminate information into the public arena.

We ask the Longel Foundation to leverage on our existing resources and instrumentation to help us create this program. We currently have funding from the government, private sector donors, and from R&D relationships with industry for our research programs, but there are no other sources of funding available, to our knowledge, to launch a combined clinical-academic effort of the magnitude proposed here.

To this end, our proposal is specifically for two phases of funding of 3 years each. The first phase is characterized by recruitments and rapid clinical and research program expansion. The second phase is characterized by continued growth and projected clinical and research self-sufficiency by Year 6.

Funding Request

The funding request should be broken down into major categories that span any major programmatic divisions of the research, if appropriate; personnel, equipment, other expenses; and project timeline per year. The funding request can be presented in text or table format, depending on the complexity of information, with table format preferable for complex material. For example,

Funding Request
Table 1 summarizes the allocation of personnel to this 6-year program, as well as programmatic and renovation costs:

	Phase I			Phase II		
	Year 1	Year 2	Year 3	Year 4	Year 5	Year 6
Personnel						
Professor, PI	40%	30%	30%	30%	30%	30%
Associate professor, co-PI	30%	30%	30%	30%	30%	30%
Assistant professor (new)		100%	50%	50%	25%	25%
Assistant professor (new)			100%	100%	50%	50%
Research scientist (new)		100%	100%	50%	50%	50%
Nurse coordinator	50%	50%	100%	100%	100%	100%
Postdoctoral fellows	50%	50%@2	50%@2	50%@2	50%@2	50%@2
Students	50%@3	50%@3	50%@3	50%@3	50%@3	50%@3
Administrative support	100%	100%	150%	200%	200%	200%
Programmatic support	$250K	$250K	$150K	$50K		
Renovation	$250K					

Budget Justification

The PI will direct this program at 40% effort in Year 1, and at 30% thereafter. The extra 10% in Year 1 accounts for the additional time expected for start-up of the program. The co-PI will dedicate 30% time to this work. New faculty and scientists will be hired during Years 2 to 4. The level of support for them begins at 100% and then decreases as they obtain independent funding. A nurse coordinator is requested at 50% effort in Years 1 and 2, and then at 100% effort as the activity and number of clinical trials increase. One 2-year postdoctoral fellow is requested for Year 1, and then two fellows per year for 2 years are requested for each year thereafter. Three graduate students are requested at 50% for each year of the program. Administrative support increases from 1 FTE to 2 FTEs by Year 4, when the program is fully operational. The request for programmatic funding (i.e., computers, animals costs, supplies) escalates as the new faculty are recruited, and then decreases in the fifth and sixth years. Renovation of existing shell space in Year 1 will provide offices for the new faculty.

By contrast, a simpler funding request may be summarized narratively. For example:

The budget requested will cover salaries for the principal investigator at 25% effort per year, two co-investigators at 20% time per year, and a postdoctoral fellow at 50% per year. The budget includes benefits at 28% and institutional overhead at 15%.

Summary of the Vision

The final summary should be used to reiterate the major attributes of the proposed work: need, suitability of the proposing team, and the team's commitment. The final statement—the vision—should be a persuasive argument for the impact that the work will have in both the short-and long-term. For example:

Summary
We are excited about the possibility of creating a major multidisciplinary program in epilepsy and improving patient care through carefully integrated clinical and research activities. We have a strong track record of success in our past work, and are eager to recruit new people and expand our resources and programs. With this grant from the Longel Foundation, we will be able to establish an integrated program of unsurpassed talent and dedication in epilepsy on the West Coast.

TABLE OF CONTENTS

Consistency in wording and accuracy of page numbering are the two key features of a good table of contents. If the structure for a table of contents is already provided by a prospective sponsor, then accurate page numbering is the only issue (assuming that the wording for sections and subsections follows the wording in the table of contents precisely). If the design of the table of contents is at the discretion of the researcher, then it should be constructed for easy reading and easy visual matching with sections in the proposal itself. Again, the wording for section and subsection headings should be identical to the wording in the table of contents.

For example,

(Title of Proposal: Clip Repair of Arteriovenous Malformations)

    I.   Introduction
   II.   Rationale for Work Proposed
        1. Incidence and medical relevance
        2. Current treatment approaches
        3. Impact of treatment on neuropsychological function
  III.   Methods
        1. Technical Development
            a. Materials selection
            b. Testing and validation
        2. Clinical Testing
            a. Clip efficacy
            b. Neuropsychological behavior
  IV.   Significance
   V.   Bibliographies of Key Personnel

BUDGETING STRATEGIES

The budget is the financial reflection of the scientific plan. Budgets may be requested in a preset format, or free form. Either way, they must be perfect. Guidelines and recommendations for how to construct and present rational budgets are presented here. A sample budget justification follows.

Budgeting for Personnel

The level of effort of each member of the research team must be driven, foremost, by the nature of the work proposed. Effort is usually calculated as a percent of a 40-hour week. Although 40 hours may be an underestimation of the time actually worked per week, it is an administrative standard. The best way to answer questions about the level of effort and the time needed to carry out the work is by carefully mapping out the proposal aims on a timeline, and considering what the work will take to complete per week (in hours) and over how many weeks. As a general rule, percent effort should be specified only for personnel for whom salary support is requested. If salary support is not requested, it is usually best to indicate effort as "as needed." Personnel should be named, whenever possible. The place holder *"To be Named"* may be used judiciously for noncore personnel who have still to be hired.

Core Personnel

Principal Investigator(s). The PI's budgeted effort should take into account the work to be done, the administrative activities that accompany this level of responsibility, and an overall commitment to the work. Even with the support of a strong working group, a small PI effort that appears to underestimate the demands of a project will limit the enthusiasm of reviewers and that of other people in decision-making positions at a sponsoring agency. Similarly, requested effort that is too high given the work proposed will also suggest poor conceptualization and planning.

For project-based research and SBIRs, 15% is generally a minimum recommended level of effort to cover both scientific and administrative responsibilities. If a PI cannot devote sufficient effort to a project because of other research commitments, then the project must either be reformulated and scaled down, or the P.I.'s effort on one or more other funded grants must be restructured. On the upper end, it is also important to consider that effort on a single research grant that is greater than 40% to 50% may limit the pursuit of other projects and sources of salary support, particularly of the PI. As a general rule, however, it is preferable to participate on fewer funded projects at a higher percent effort on each (e.g., minimally 10%), than on many projects with only a token (i.e., 1% to 5%) level of effort. The rationale is that productivity is typically commensurate with commitment, and that many relatively minor commitments are more likely to clutter an individual's research program than advance it.

On training grants, fellowships, and scholarships, a minimum effort of 50% to 70% is usually required. This is consistent with the expectation that the individual will be primarily, if not fully, dedicated to the program.

Investigators. As for PIs, the percent effort for other investigators should be driven by the work proposed. The choice of investigators should be made on the basis of the specific requirements of the research, and the percent effort should be driven by the responsibilities associated with those requirements. Unlike PIs, there is no recommended minimum or maximum effort but, again, effort must be calculated on a 40-hour work week, and over a given number of weeks if less than 52, or per year. It is entirely reasonable to request support for investigators for one year and not for another, or to vary the level of requested support based on the specific aims of the project and the work schedule. Investigators may fall into any one of several generally equivalent classifications (e.g., co-investigator, investigator, associated investigator), usually based on the administrative rules of the host institution rather than on differentation based on scientific need.

Collaborators. As described in chapter 2, collaborators are individuals within the PI's organization who play a very specific role on a project and who have an interest in the outcome of the work. As in the case of investigators, collaborator effort must be driven by the amount of work the individual will do, calculated for each year separately, and only for those years in which the collaborative work will actually occur.

Adjunct Personnel

Adjunct Professional Personnel and Consultants.
There is a wide range of professional personnel who provide scientific, technical, and administrative support to a project. Their effort is related to specific functions on a project, and should be budgeted accordingly. Their level of expertise, on the one hand, and their level of

involvement on the other, should determine whether they are described as key or adjunct personnel. Adjunct professional personnel and consultants bring very specific expertise to a project but have a limited commitment to the project overall. For example, a psychologist may be brought in for the first 6 months of a project to run psychometric tests for subject screening, or a pathologist may be required for a limited time to perform histology on tissue specimens. If the responsibilities and expectations of such individuals do not extend beyond a fixed period of time or fixed amount of work, assigning them the role of consultant is appropriate.

Consultants may be drawn from within an organization or from the outside. They may be paid a salary based on percent effort, a fixed salary for a fixed period of time, or an hourly wage. The most appropriate mechanism should be determined on the basis of the needs of the project and the negotiated requirements of the consultant. Some sponsors set limits on the amount that can be paid hourly to consultants; this should be considered carefully in constructing a budget for them.

Research Associates and Assistants. Research associates and assistants provide a valuable support function. Research associates are typically drawn from a more senior and well-trained pool than research assistants. Allocation of responsibilities to the research associates and expectations of them should be commensurate with experience, as should the responsibilities allocated to research assistants, who will require greater supervision.

Students. Predoctoral and postdoctoral students can both provide valuable input to a project and benefit from the training associated with it. In addition to the actual work conducted, postdoctoral students may also help supervise the work of predoctoral students. As for all other personnel, the allocation of time must be based on the work they will do and the contributions they will make to the project. The designation of postdoctoral fellows as key personnel is dependent on their level of expertise. Graduate students are generally not regarded as key personnel on a research proposal even though they may be crucial to the actual work.

Administrative Personnel. Administrative support is usually not an area that can be provided through federal grant funding today, except through funding for large scale programs in which the administration forms a fundamental component of the infrastructure. Administrative support is relatively easier to procure from nonfederal grants and contracts, however, and when allowed as a budgetary item, the allocation should be determined in the same way as for other personnel: specific duties, based on a 40-hour work week, and averaged out over a 12-month period for each year of the proposal period.

Budgeting for Nonpersonnel Items

Travel. Requests for travel costs must carefully follow the specifications of the sponsor because some will only support travel for key personnel, others only for domestic travel, and so on. On major project-based proposals (exceeding $100,000 per year), it is reasonable to request two trips per year: one for the PI and one for one of the other core members of the research team. Costs for travel should be based on specific estimates of the cost of transportation, lodging, and food at the time that the proposal is being formulated. It is not necessary to present these data specifically, unless requested by the sponsor.

Equipment. Equipment can be requested if it is an allowable budget item, and is necessary for the completion of the work. The budget justification should specify why the equipment is needed; for example, it is not currently part of the laboratory's resources and cannot be reasonably borrowed from another laboratory. The choice of a given piece of equipment should also be justified with respect to alternatives, especially if an alternative is substantially less expensive. In the case of equipment upgrades, it is important to be explicit about how the upgrade is critical to the completion of the work, such as sufficient computer memory for data acquisition. All requests for major equipment should be backed up by a quotation from the vendor if possible.

Other Research Expenses. Many other research costs, such as reimbursement to volunteers, purchase and housing of laboratory animals, and costs for use of specialized equipment should be budgeted precisely according to the research plan on a yearly basis (or less, if the project is less than 52 weeks in duration). These data are best represented in a spreadsheet format for easy appreciation, as shown here:

	Year 1	*Year 2*	*Year 3*
	50 volunteers x $10/hr x 3 hrs	48 volunteers x $10/hr x 3 hrs	45 volunteers x $10/hr x 3 hrs
	$50 first-time payment for participation		
Total subject costs	**$4,000**	**$1,440**	**$1,350**

Justification of subject costs
Fifty subjects will be recruited to the initial subject pool for this longitudinal study that involves 3 hours of participation per subject per year. Based on prior experience, we expect that 2% of the subjects will drop out each year, and this is reflected in the change in number of subjects from 50 to 48 to 45 from Year 1 through Year 3 who will need to be reimbursed.

Miscellaneous Costs. Miscellaneous costs such as telephone and publication expenses are acceptable as long as they are properly justified and not specifically excluded by the sponsor. For example, toll or long-distance costs for a collaborator at a remote site is an obviously justifiable cost, as is the cost of color illustrations in publications that must be borne by the authors.

Budget Justification

The budget must translate into a detailed budget justification. There is no leniency in the system for unjustified items, and if they are unjustified, they may be cut. An example of a complete budget justification follows:

Budget Justification

We propose to implement and validate a new cross-linguistic battery of tests for the evaluation of aphasia. The project draws on the unique personnel and facilities assembled at the Center for Language Studies at Longhorn. The technical and clinical skills of the group, the multilingual patient population and the resources at the associated Stroke Center provide an outstanding opportunity for success of this project. This opportunity exists, to the best of our knowledge, at no other medical center in the world.

Three years of funding is projected to cover the scope of the proposed project.

Personnel:

Michelle J. Tarwin, PhD (principal investigator, professor of neurology and neurological sciences) *has extensive experience in the development, implementation and evaluation of new assessment techniques for language disorders and is a recognized leader in the field. She will coordinate and direct all aspects of this research program, manage all budgetary matters, and prepare reports documenting progress. She will have personal responsibility for directing and defining the development of the methods, and will work closely with the other members of the research team.*

Marti Jied, MD (co-principal investigator, assistant professor of neurology and neurological sciences) *is co-director of the Longhorn Stroke Center and has extensive experience in the clinical and neurological aspects of language acquisition and language loss, with a special emphasis on multilingualism. He will serve as the primary clinical contact for the project, and will coordinate patient recruitment. Dr. Jied's expertise will be required for all aspects of the research, and his overall effort is projected to be a half-day per week.*

Edwin Genzman, MD (investigator, assistant professor of neurology and neurological sciences) *will serve as a clinical con-*

tact for the study and will evaluate the patient data together with Dr. Jied. His expertise in the assessment of stroke is required for all aspects of the research, and his overall effort is expected to be a half-day per week.

Ida Jamestine, PhD (biostatistician, associate professor of statistics) is well known for her theoretical and applied work in biomedical applications. She will work closely with Dr. Tarwin and the other investigators on subject testing and the interpretation of the data.

To be Named (postdoctoral fellow, Department of Neurology and Neurological Sciences) will work with Dr. Tarwin to optimize and validate the battery, and with Drs. Jied, Genzman and Jamestine to acquire, collate and interpret the data.

Thiery Bouchon (consultant, Department of Speech and Hearing Sciences) is known internationally for her work in language rehabilitation. She will be leaving on sabbatical beginning in Year 2 of the study, but will be available to consult on the development and validation of the battery on a limited basis of 20 hours per week in the first year. Her insight will be invaluable for the success of this project.

Salaries inflate at a rate of 5% per year.

Supplies: Miscellaneous supply and publications costs are projected to be $1,000 per year.

Equipment: A Pentium-II based computer is requested to enable processing of the large amount of data to be collected. A quotation from the vendor follows. Currently available computers cannot be used because they are fully dedicated to clinical database management.

Travel: Funds are requested for one domestic trip for the principal investigator to present the research results at a national scientific meeting.

Summary

Budgeting for research is both a science based on known requirements, and an art in terms of strategic planning. It is important, therefore, to create an initial budget only after the specific aims have been delineated, and if the research will involve a complex series of experiments, to wait until the associated experimental plan is complete. The risk, otherwise, is a budget that either adversely limits the work you wish to do or that, alternatively, is unrealistically high.

It is equally important to revisit the initial budget as the proposal evolves. Be sure, for example, that 25 hours of computed tomography (CT) scan time are not inadvertently planned for a 24-hour day, or that an animal model is not expected to produce a litter of six offspring every month for reasonable statistical power when the species only produces two offspring twice a year. Even in the case of modular budgets in which the sponsor does not require an actual budget breakdown but only a budget classification (e.g., $50,000, $100,000), it is necessary to calculate the actual costs of the project both for the purposes of correctly estimating the classification and for future project execution. Finally, always consider the bottom line dollar amount. It may be perfect, or it may be out of balance—too high or too low—with respect to the desire or funding ability of a prospective sponsor. When out of balance, the options are either to seek a new sponsor, or to stay with the same sponsor but reevaluate the budgeting strategy and reconfigure the science until the two converge.

RESEARCH ENVIRONMENT

The description of the research environment should focus initially on the primary existing resources available to carry out the work, separated from other supporting resources. The primary resources include, as appropriate for each proposal, the clinical environment from which patients will be drawn, laboratory facilities, major equipment, animal care facilities, computing resources, and office space.

Secondary resources are the resources that exist in the surrounding environment, but are not needed for the work per se. Evidence that the overall environment is robust is a valuable asset, however. Therefore, space permitting, these supporting resources should also be identified and described.

In this section of the proposal, do not include resources that will be acquired through the grant or the proposed work. Reserve this information for the budget justification, as described previously.

PROFESSIONAL AND FUNDING HISTORY OF CORE PERSONNEL

The compendium of curricula vitae or biographical sketches and other support material exhibit both the credibility and fundability of the researcher.

Professional History

The presentation of the professional history of each key person is typically required as either an abbreviated (usually two pages) curriculum vitae (CV) or as a biographical sketch.

Abbreviated Curriculum Vitae. The abbreviated CV should provide a full listing of the investigator's educational background (i.e., schools attended and degrees earned), professional background (i.e., employment history), and professional accomplishments (e.g., honors and awards, patents, professional service in societies, journal review). If the professional service is lengthy, it should be customized to represent the service that is most relevant to the work proposed. Similarly, if a full listing of publications would exceed allowable space, then the list should be customized to emphasize the competence of the researcher for work proposed and the match with the sponsor. Competence will be measured in terms of previous relevant publications in peer-reviewed journals; a match with a sponsor will be measured by awards, patents, and publications in areas of mutual interest. When the sections call only for selected information, they should be identified as such (e.g., *Selected Awards and Honors, Representative Publications*). This is a distinctly better strategy than attempting to crowd too much information into a small space with a miniscule font and nonexistent margins and rendering the text virtually unreadable.

A standard format for the abbreviated CV appears on page 124.

Biographical Sketches. Unlike the CV, the biographical sketch is a narrative description of the accomplishments of each investigator. It should be written as a careful integration of the chronology of accomplishments and the highlights of historical and contemporary accomplishments most relevant to the proposed work.

Boris T. Tilren, MD

Education

University of Hawon 1988 BS Chemistry
University of Minneta 1992 MD Neurology

Research and Professional Experience

1987–1988 Research Assistant, University of Hawon,
Department of Chemistry, with Dr. K. Liu
1993–1997 University of Minneta, Resident, Neurology
1997–1998 San Diego Medical Center, Fellow, Neurology
1998–present Assistant Professor, San Diego Medical Center,
Dept. of Neurology

Academic Awards and Honors

1988 Summa Cum Laude, University of Hawon
1988 First Prize, Darlinger Undergraduate Research Award
1997 Chief Resident, University of Minneta, Neurology
1998 Best Poster, American Academy of Neurology

Selected Publications and Presentations (of a total of 62)

Liu, K., Des, E., Briel, J.J., Dende, J.B., Tilren, B. (1992). Advanced
neurochemical analysis of experimentally induced neurofibrillary tangles in
the temporal cortex, *Annals of Neurological Sciences*, 4(20), pp. 367–388.

Tilren, B., Edias T., (1993). Development of a modified tetramethyl
benzadine tissue staining technique. *Proceedings of the Histological Society
of North America*, 6(Supp. 3), p. 121.

Examples of three narrative biographical sketches follow here:

(Brief: Senior Investigator)

Jennifer H. Frynd, PhD (professor of psychology) is the director of the Aging and Alcoholism Studies Laboratory. She has been instrumental in the development and implementation of new technologies for diagnosis and therapy of aging and alcoholism-related disorders and brings fundamental knowledge and invaluable experience in multimodal techniques to the program. Dr. Frynd has held numerous federal and nonfederal research grants and contracts. She is currently principal investigator on an NIH P50 Center Grant on Physiological Processes in Neurodegenerative Disease (National Institute on Aging), and is co-principal investigator with Dr. H. Maxiffe on a pending NINDS RO1 grant on anxiety and alcoholism. Dr. Frynd has won numerous teaching awards throughout her career, and is highly respected among her colleagues both nationally and worldwide.

(In-depth: Senior Investigator)
Dr. Eugene Swift became chairman of Pamard University's Department of Psychiatry in September 1991. He is known internationally for his work in psychiatric evaluation of eating disorders, and his current interests are focused on anorexia and bulimia in adolescents.

Dr. Swift received his MD from Reserve West University in 1976. He was nominated an American Psychiatric Association Fellow during his fellowship at Reserve West, and joined the faculty there as an assistant professor and director of the Eating Disorders Unit in 1981. He quickly rose through the academic ranks and was appointed full professor in 1987. In 1992, he co-founded the inpatient psychiatric center for treatment and research, which earned recognition as a national research resource with a major award from the National Institute of Mental Health.

Dr. Swift has published more than 200 papers and book chapters in psychiatry, and he authored Staging of Eating Disorders in 1986 (Naver & Associates, Publishers). He is on numerous national committees, including the Executive Committee of the Association of University Psychiatrists, was elected as a foreign member to the British Royal College of Psychiatry in 1984 and sits on many advisory committees to the industry. He provides editorial service to more than 10 national and international professional journals and has been on the editorial boards of leading journals in the discipline, including Psychiatry (associate editor).

Dr. Swift has received substantial peer-reviewed funding for his research since 1983. For example, a prestigious early investigator award from the American Psychological Association and NIH (NIMH) dealt with depression associated with eating disorders. Currently he serves as the PI of the Reserve West component of an NIMH-funded multicenter consortium on obsessive compulsive disorders.

Dr. Swift has served as a mentor and co-sponsor for several young academic psychiatrists—for example, Jane Aton and Kaumi Jersi—who themselves have become leaders in the field. Dr. Swift also won the Outstanding Teacher Award at Reserve West four times. Dr. Swift's vision and dedication to academic psychiatry have been essential ingredients in his ability to draw outstanding scientists and clinicians to this program, and to place it at the forefront of the field in the United States today.

(Junior Investigator)
John R. Lee, PhD received his BA in education from Colma College in 1986, and a PhD in human biology from Stanbridge University in 1993. Currently, Dr. Lee is a postdoctoral fellow at Stanbridge, working in conjunction with Dr. Grover Phills on early developmental problems in autism. His experience both in education and in the biological basis of human behavior is an invaluable asset to this project.

Sponsors such as foundations sometimes require full CVs, although this is relatively uncommon since CVs can grow to significant lengths over the course of an investigator's career. Nevertheless, the opportunity has both advantages and disadvantages. On the one hand, a full CV and the all-encompassing information can provide an impressive view of a person's accomplishments. On the other, it does not specifically portray the quality of the match of a researcher to a project and sponsor, which can be a drawback if that match is not unequivocally clear.

Funding History

Sponsors are generally most comfortable providing support to researchers who have a track record of success and, ideally, some funding record. Each sponsor has its own specific requirements for how this information should be conveyed, but irrespective of the format, the main aspects of this information are the title of other grants, role on project, percent effort, funding period, funding amount, and a statement about the goals of the grants and whether there is any overlap with the one proposed. These should be grouped into active grants and pending grants, as appropriate.

For researchers whose programs are varied, it is also often useful to group active and pending support so that support that is relevant to the current proposal is clearly separated from the rest. This is an especially good strategy when a sponsor is seeking to support an investigator who is not well-funded in one area, but has significant funding in others. A brief narrative justification and a grouped list can very effective. For example:

To date, the primary focus of my research has been on improved methods of 18 FDG PET imaging. Although this work has been very successful (two NIH grants and several publications), during the past 2 years I have also become interested in the capabilities of SPECT imaging. Toward this end, I initiated pilot research in healthy young and schizophrenic volunteer subjects. Preliminary results from this work are described in Section C.2. The purpose of this seed grant application is to provide the foundation for formalizing this new research direction and expanding my area of expertise. The successful completion of the proposed project will assist me in establishing the needed track record for future research efforts and extramural grant applications in the area of SPECT imaging.

Grants related to schizophrenia

Active

   None

Pending

   Present grant

Grants related to the neurochemistry of mood disorders

Active

Institutional seed grant: Basis of Mood Shift

   Jody Crish, PhD, principal investigator (25% effort)

   $15,000 total direct costs

   Project period: 9/1/97–8/31/99

NIMH R29MH 66745

Neurochemistry and Mood Behavior

Jody Crish, PhD, principal investigator (10% effort)

$349,999 total direct costs

Project period: 7/1/97–6/30/02

There are mechanisms in place at many agencies to serve the needs of first time investigators with no history of funding. It is important to capitalize on these opportunities to build up a funding record.

Because active other support is a time-varying phenomenon, NIH has adopted a "just-in-time" policy for certain grants. In this case, documentation of the funding history for each investigator is requested only when a grant is likely to fund. This policy has both intrinsic advantages and disadvantages. The primary advantage is that it is efficient to submit funding information only once (i.e., at the time that it is relevant and coincident with the actual funding of a grant, rather than at the beginning of a review cycle, which can take as long as 9 months). The disadvantage is that reviewers may be interested in the overall fundability and track record of a researcher, but under this new policy, that information is no longer available at the time of review.

HUMAN AND ANIMAL
USE COMPLIANCE

All sponsors require assurance that the protocols proposed for using animals or human subjects are approved by institutional authorities. Universities and large organizations have standing institutional review boards for human use, and panels for review of animal use. Review boards are composed of both researchers and lay people who work together to ensure oversight of both scientific and humanitarian aspects of the research. Several entities exist around the United States to provide independent services to organizations that are not large enough to have their own review boards. Their services can be contracted either on a protocol-by-protocol basis, or for specified periods of time.

The major issues for animal use are appropriateness of the choice of species, appropriateness of the protocol in terms of experimental efficiency, and humane care.

The major issues for the use of humans are nature of the population, including inclusion and exclusion criteria such as age group and gender, recruitment plans; subject confidentiality; potential hazard; and risks versus benefits of participation.

When developing these sections, it is imperative to address each of these issues specifically, as appropriate. Protocols and consent forms require very specific formats and wordings, and review boards may take as long as 6 to 8 weeks for approvals. Planning ahead is key, particularly when, for certain sponsors, approval is needed at the time of proposal submission.

LETTERS OF SUPPORT

Letters of support from collaborators and consultants signify their agreement to participate in the research as proposed. For some sponsors, such letters are a requirement; for other sponsors, they are optional. In either case, if they are included, they should contain the following elements:

- A statement about the overall importance of the research proposed.
- A statement indicating the willingness to participate.
- Evidence of the expertise of the outside resource.
- A statement indicating the parameters of participation, such as percent effort and responsibilities.

For example:

Dear Dr. Von de Seep,

Thank you very much for the opportunity to collaborate with you on your research on Pain Management in Aging. Your track record in pain research since 1990 has been superb, and I am confident that the results of the proposed continuing work will be equally substantial. In fact, the work directly complements my own research on the development of back pain in middle-aged men and women.

As we discussed, I will refer patients to your study, and assist in interpretation of the data throughout the project. My effort will be on an as needed basis, with no salary support.

Good luck in obtaining funding for this highly worthy project.

Sincerely,

Judith Artle, MD, Director, Back Pain Center

SUMMARY

The overall critical features of the administrative sections are clarity of presentation in terms of conceptual consistency, logic, and meticulous presentation. The key features of the individual sections are summarized in Table 7.1.

TABLE 7.1
Key Features of Administrative Sections

Administrative Sections	*Key Features*
Proposal title	Brevity
	Understandability
Key words	Specificity
Cover page	Accuracy
Technical abstract	Clearly stated goals and deliverables
	Technical accuracy
	Projections for anticipated outcome
	in near and long-term
General abstract	Clearly stated goals and deliverables
	Broadly defined methodological approach
	Absence of jargon
	Projections of anticipated benefit
Executive summary	Conciseness
	Completeness

TABLE 7.1 (Continued)

Administrative Sections	Key Features
Table of contents	Accuracy Consistency in wording of titles and subtitles
Budget	Personnel allocations and programmatic (direct research) needs based strictly on the scientific plan Strong justification of all itemized costs Accuracy of calculations
Research environment	Evidence that resources exist to support the work Separation of primary resources required to carry out the work from other secondary supporting resources
Professional and funding history of core personnel	Completeness Accuracy Separation of funding for projects relevant to current proposal from projects not directly related
Human and animal use compliance	Careful attention to sponsor's requirements Strong justification for use of selected living models Clarity and thoroughness
Letters of support	Accuracy (e.g., the letter should use the correct title of the proposal) Specificity in terms of purpose (e.g., supporting the work or committing to carry out work) Enthusiasm

Chapter 8

Preliminary and Ancillary Pragmatic Steps to Proposal Submission

The strategic position of a research proposal can be strengthened through early contact with a potential sponsor, submission of appendices and supplemental material, and inclusion of a cover letter with the proposal. This chapter discusses these various opportunities in terms of their significance and timing.

PRELIMINARY COMMUNICATION WITH A SPONSOR

Once a first pass through the relevant conceptualization pathway is completed, direct communication with a sponsor can be advantageous in terms of refining a research idea and developing the proposal. In some cases, such as multicomponent programs, it is a requirement. Personal communication typically occurs with a program manager with whom the quality of the match between the research idea that is being formulated and the program's priorities and interests can be explored.

Although a program manager can never make any guarantees about the fundability of an idea, initial contact either by telephone, in writing, or through personal contact such as at a professional meeting can provide insight into the way the proposal will need to be developed to be the most competitive and can lead to an understanding of how close to or far it is from meeting the program goals. Beyond published program descriptions, the discussion may also be revealing in terms of the sponsor's overall track record and predisposition to funding different categories of researchers and research. Sponsors may have a preference, for example, for funding junior versus senior researchers, MDs versus PhDs, projects versus programs, or even cellular versus systems research. Finally, the discussion will be valuable bilaterally in creating the sense for the researcher that the audience is people, not just an amorphous organization, and in conveying to the sponsor that the research team is worthy of the sponsor's consideration. Ideally, the initial contact will be the first in a long-term relation that involves scientific and programmatic success of mutual benefit.

LETTER OF INTENT, NONCOMPETITIVE PREPROPOSALS, AND COMPETITIVE PREPROPOSALS

Preliminary contact in the form of written material may be a letter of intent, a noncompetitive preproposal, or a competitive preproposal. These types of communication are largely unidirectional, from investigator to program manager. By contrast to the feedback that can be elicited from preliminary discussions, feedback other than the binary decision to invite or not invite a full proposal is typically not provided.

Letter of Intent

The letter of intent is submitted to signify an investigator's intention to respond to a program announcement. It serves to assist the program manager in anticipating the review workload and in setting up review groups. The letter should include the title of the proposal, the title of the program announcement, and if appropriate, the name of the PI, investigators, affiliations and correspondence information. Failure to submit this material usually does not preclude the submission of a full proposal unless stated otherwise in the program announcement, but may bias the review of the proposal.

Preproposals

Many sponsors request brief preproposals, also referred to as concept papers, for review before full proposals are invited. In some cases, the preproposals are noncompetitive in that they are reviewed for their suitability to the sponsor, with all matches accepted. The match will be determined on the basis of the suitability of the PI to the program and research concept. In other cases, preproposals are judged competitively, with only a proportion accepted for further consideration. In either case, all preproposals should follow the conceptualization and preparation guidelines for a full proposal.

Preproposals should include subsections with specific objectives, background information, an argument for significance, evidence of prior work, and hypotheses with methods. As with full proposals, they should be consistent and rigorous throughout. A unique feature of preproposals is the need for a section that explicitly addresses the perceived match with a sponsor and the sponsor's priority as described in a program announcement or other published material. Unless instructed otherwise, this section should appear last and either stand alone or be embodied within the summary to the text. For example:

> *We will respond to the Foundation's goal to improve pediatric health care for children by developing a program in outcomes research that is specifically focused on the sensitivity, specificity and cost-effectiveness of new technology developed for children. Our program will incorporate both qualitative and quantitative methods in an environment that promotes the routine and rapid transfer of new technology to clinical care.*

Preproposals for training funds also commonly require a statement about career objectives. This section should be an abbreviated version of a fully developed career statement, as described in chapter 3, and should follow the same guidelines.

Although preproposals are often as challenging to compose conceptually as full proposals, they are always less cumbersome because they are a fraction of the length. The preproposal process is reasonably humane, therefore, in that only researchers with truly competitive proposals are invited to submit full proposals, sparing researchers with noncompetitive ones from fruitless activity. On the average, sponsors will invite between 10% and 30% of preproposals to be submitted as full proposals. The timing between acceptance of a preproposal and the submission of the full proposal is usually 30 to 60 days. This interim period is an opportune time to collect more preliminary data and to reevaluate and refine the concepts for the eventual full submission.

APPENDICES AND SUPPLEMENTAL INFORMATION

Appendices

Certain sponsors allow supporting scientific information in the form of appendices to accompany the submission of proposals. Such material may include reprints of published material, preprints, raw data for which the summary data are presented in the text, videotapes, and large-scale illustrations or images that allow more detail to be appreciated than in a reduced version in the text. It is essential that the material does not provide primary information so as to appear to circumvent the page limitations for the body of the text; therefore, elaborate discussions of methodology, background or prior work, for example, are generally not acceptable.

A set of appendices should have its own table of contents, and each component should be clearly labeled. For example:

Appendices

Appendix A: *Reprints (Stone et al., 1997; Geshack and Stone, 1997)*
Appendix B: *Clinical Scoring Sheets (Sheets 1–3)*
Appendix C: *Original Images (Figures 1–7)*

The appendices should be assembled in the order to which the material is referred in the text. If there is no reference to an appendix in the text, the appendix should not be included.

Supplemental Information

In some circumstances, information in the form of a supplement can be submitted after the proposal deadline. It is appropriate to submit supplemental information after receiving permission from the program manager to whom the original proposal was submitted, and when a truly significant result in support of the work proposed has been obtained since the submission date. It is also appropriate to seek permission for a supplement when a significant error is discovered and the supplemental information is needed to restore accuracy. Submission of supplementary information should be reserved for the most definitive results or egregious errors (in other words, only material that impacts the review of the scientific content), because acceptance of the material for use in review will be at the program manager's discretion.

In addition, for the benefit of the reviewers—and ultimately to promote a favorable disposition to a proposal—the amount of supplemental material should be kept to a minimum, clearly linked to the relevant sections in the proposal, and presented succinctly.

The key information describing the supplement should be conveyed in a cover letter, with accompanying material attached. For example:

Dear Ms. Lion,

Thank you for the opportunity to submit this supplemental information in support of our proposal <u>Prospective Planning in Patients with Prefrontal Pathology</u>.

First, we wish to report that we have recently discovered a new type of prospective planning anomaly in patients with prefrontal pathology that has not previously been reported in the literature. This is described in detail in the attached manuscript, just submitted to <u>Brain and Language</u>.

Second, we noted an error in Table 4 on page 58 of the proposal, where correlation values were inadvertently referred to as median scores. We regret this error.

We include here four copies (one copy for each reviewer) of the corrected page for substitution into the proposal and four copies of the manuscript. We would be grateful if you could pass this material on to the reviewers.

Thank you very much.

Sincerely,

Chip Doak, PhD

Despite the need for caution, do not hesitate to seek permission to submit supplemental material if you have it. Submitting corrections is unlikely to affect the outcome of a proposal significantly, but outstanding new data can indeed favorably change the fate of a review.

COVER LETTERS

A simple cover letter that transmits the proposal to a sponsor is always a proper attachment. It should include the title of the proposal and the program announcement to which it is responsive, if any, and the list of investigators. At the PI's discretion, it may also include a summary of the project timeline and budget.

For proposals to the NIH, it affords an opportunity to suggest the assignment to one of the institutes and study sections (also referred to as initial review groups; IRGs). For example:

Dear Dr. Chanson,

In response to RFA 9800556, please find enclosed my proposal Acalculia Following Stroke. The research is projected for a 3-year period, and will be conducted by myself, co-PI Dr. Ralph Trall, a clinical neuropsychologist (Department of Psychiatry and Behavioral Sciences), and co-investigators Drs. Sharon Abbot and Garrett Drow, both accomplished stroke researchers from the Department of Physical Medicine and Rehabilitation.

We feel that the goals of the work will be of greatest interest to the National Institute of Neurologic Diseases and Stroke. In addition, given the nature of this work, we would like to request that our proposal be assigned to the Neurology A study section, where we believe the expertise to review this proposal is most likely to be represented.

Please do not hesitate to contact me should you require any further information.

Thank you very much for your time and attention.

Sincerely,

Janet Stone, MD, PhD

Cover letters also provide an opportunity to recommend special reviewers if a proposal covers a highly specialized field, as well as to request the exclusion of certain reviewers in the case of perceived conflict of interest.

SUMMARY

The ancillary pragmatic steps to proposal development require relatively small investments of time and effort compared to actual conceptualization and preparation time, and can have a high pay-off. The key features of the various steps are summarized in Table 8.1. These opportunities should be used prudently and wisely, with the goal of maximizing the quality and fairness of review for all parties involved in the prospective funding relation.

TABLE 8.1
Key Features of Preliminary and Ancillary Steps
to Proposal Submission

Preliminary and Ancillary Steps	Key Features
Preliminary communication with a sponsor	Identification of the strength of the match between the *researcher* and the *sponsor.* Identification of the goodness of the match between the *research* and the *sponsor's* interests. Identification of the sponsor's priorities and track record. Personal communication of the worthiness of the research team.
Letters of intent, noncompetitive preproposals, competitive preproposals	Concise communication of research and administrative plan. Scientific rigor. Demonstration of an explicit match with sponsor.
Supplemental information	Transmission of significant new information (since proposal submission) critical to the review. Correction of egregious errors. Brevity.
Cover letters	Personal transmission of the work. Recommendation for review expertise. Reviewer inclusion/exclusion.

Chapter 9

Reviews, Resubmissions, and Rebuttals

Proposal review usually has at least three major junctures that, depending on the size of the sponsor, are crossed formally or informally. These junctures are sponsor acceptance of the proposal, scientific peer review, and proposal selection by sponsor.

This chapter is concerned with proposals for which funding is not likely given an unfavorable outcome at any one of these junctures, and for which an understanding of the review process and the mind set of reviewers is especially important to eventual success. Chapter 10 and 11 are dedicated to the favorable outcome of review—when funding is successfully achieved—and the goal is to successfully maintain and nurture a funding relationship with a sponsor.

THE REVIEW PROCESS

Sponsor Acceptance of a Proposal

Logging Incoming Proposals. The first administrative step by the sponsor includes logging of all incoming proposals. While the size of a sponsor's internal review staff can be expected to be proportional to the size of the sponsor and the anticipated number of applications, the load may still be significant. Confirmation of receipt of a proposal is not necessarily made pro forma therefore, and if a confirmation is supplied, it may not be sent out closely time-locked to the proposal receipt date. It is wise to telephone or e-mail a sponsor promptly following a deadline to track the proposal and ensure that it has reached its intended destination.

Proposal Triage. The second step in the administrative acceptance of a proposal is the triage by the sponsor to eliminate proposals that do not conform to the application instructions (although some sponsors will contact researchers and allow them to correct relatively minor errors, such as an improperly formatted reference section or an omitted letter of collaboration), and to categorize the proposals for assignment to appropriate reviewers and review groups.

Given the importance of the triage step to the fate of a proposal, it is essential to be alert to its outcome. For example, it may be possible to persuade a sponsor who would not necessarily accept a corrected version of a returned proposal to do so. As another example (see also chapter 8), it may be necessary to request that the category of expertise to which the proposal has been assigned be changed because it is either incorrect or suboptimal. Time is of the essence, however: a quick response with strong backing can have good success; a sluggish response is not likely to be received favorably.

REVIEWERS AND SCIENTIFIC REVIEW

Reviewers

Sponsors are committed to the areas they have chosen to serve and are, therefore, extremely serious about the selection of their reviewers. Sponsors commonly select reviewers from among those whom they have already funded, but expertise may be sought from outside this group as well.

In general, reviewers have the following in common:

- Expertise in their respective disciplines (although their expertise may not be as detailed as the PI's on a specific subject).
- Relevant funded projects or programs.
- Busy schedules.

Because service in review has little tangible return, many reviewers would rather be conducting their own research, writing their own proposals, or having personal time than reviewing other people's grants. Consider that a review of a single proposal may take as long as 12 hours, not to mention days spent participating in review meetings when that is a requirement. Other than reimbursement for travel, honoraria are also usually minimal or nonexistent. Nevertheless, service as a reviewer is an expectation that accompanies successful funding and represents a milestone in a research career: To be invited is an honor. Moreover, it allows for a glimpse of new research directions that can be useful in the formulation of new ideas, and is an opportunity to shape the direction and future of research in a discipline.

Scientific Review and Proposal Evaluation

Scientific review will yield one of four possible outcomes. Ranging from the most negative to the most positive:

1. The proposal receives a review that does not allow it to be eligible for funding, and further pursuit of the proposed direction is discouraged either implicitly or explicitly.
2. The proposal receives a review that does not render it eligible for funding, but further attempt to achieve funding through proposal revision is encouraged.
3. The research is considered meritorious, but the proposal does not receive a review that unequivocally places it above the funding payline. In this category, the strength of the match of the proposal concept with the sponsor's priority is crucial since a sponsor can exercise discretion here in determining which proposals it will fund, and which will need to be revised and resubmitted.
4. The proposal receives a review that unequivocally places it above the funding payline (see next chapter).

Although not all sponsors provide extensive written reviews to PIs, most provide at least some minimal feedback based on reviewers' notes or discussion. Therefore, feedback may come simply as part of a letter that indicates the final funding decision with some comments transcribed verbatim or paraphrased. For example:

> *Dear Dr. Roses,*
>
> *We are pleased to inform you that your proposal "Cannabis in the Alleviation of Chronic Pain" has been selected for funding. It received a score of 96 on a 100 point scale. Reviewer comments were unanimously laudatory with respect to both scientific approach and nature of the experimental design.*
>
> *We will forward details about the administrative steps needed to begin funding under separate cover within the next 30 days. Funding will start on January 1, 1999.*
>
> *Congratulations ...*

Interpretability of recommendations becomes possible with increasing extensiveness of the review. For example, when the reviewers' comments are summarized in the letter or in an attachment, extra details, like those that follow, can be revealing:

- *Likely to make an important contribution to the field.*
- *Rationale is well-developed.*
- *Interesting study design, but nitrogen-13 ammonia should be used rather than rubidium-82, since the mathematical modeling for nitrogen-13 ammonia has been better developed and validated.*

The greatest benefit is reaped from reviews that are extensive, such as from NIH, which commonly provides multipage reviews from multiple reviewers. Their newly adopted review criteria span:

- Significance of the proposed work, in terms of the problem area and the potential to advance scientific knowledge or lead to new areas of research.
- Approach, in terms of the conceptual framework of the experimental methods, including recognition of potential obstacles and alternate approaches.

- Innovation, in terms of the originality of and challenges presented by the proposed work.
- Investigator, in terms of the qualifications of the PI and the research team.
- Environment, in terms of the appropriateness and appropriate use of available resources.

This type of proposal-review exchange truly provides valuable information currency in the research development process. It is reasonable, therefore, to investigate the extent to which a sponsor provides feedback, and utilize that data point as a criterion in choosing whether or not to pursue that sponsor as a potential future source of funding.

RESUBMISSIONS

The opportunity to revise a proposal according to the review recommendations and resubmit it at an advantage over first-time submissions is an option afforded by only a handful of sponsors. Many sponsors, however, will accept revised applications for certain opportunities such as for project-based research, but at no explicit advantage over others. A minority of sponsors will not accept revised applications at all. Here, the discussion focuses on the first two types of sponsors and on resubmitting proposals to them.

The structural features common to resubmissions are a cover letter or introduction that discusses the revisions that have been made and the corresponding revisions in the body of the text and administrative sections.

The scientific feature common to resubmissions is scientific progress, in terms, at least, of refined hypotheses, design plans, or publications since the original submission. Even in the absence of extramural funding, there is an expectation that progress is being made; never make the mistake of assuming, however, that an enhanced preliminary results section is so impressive that it obviates the need for detailed experimental plans and a flawless revision.

Cover Letters and Introductions

Cover letters to revised proposals should not be too long (certainly not longer than about one page), but should contain enough detail about the revisions that have been made to a proposal so that the program manager and reviewers (assuming that the cover letter, per se, is transmitted to reviewers) can appreciate that the comments in the review were taken into consideration. As a simple example,

February 1, 1997

Dear Ms. Kilty,

*Please find enclosed our revised proposal, **Teenage Drinking Patterns**, submitted originally on June 1, 1996. We were grateful for the reviewers' thoughtful comments and their recognition of the significance of our proposed work.*

We have made every effort to address the reviewers' concerns in this revised application. In particular, we have substantially rewritten the methods section to include more detail about our procedures and data analyses. Also, given reviewers' concerns about the large volume of data we will be collecting, we have revised the budget to include an additional half-time research associate and a full-time postdoctoral fellow.

Finally, we have updated the Prior Work section to include some of our latest results related to this proposal.

Thank you very much for considering this proposal.

Sincerely,

J. Frint, MD

Director, Adolescent Medicine

The expectation for an introduction to a revised proposal—more so than for a cover letter—is that all major changes that have been made to the proposal in response to reviewers' comments are itemized and discussed. It is also important to read between the lines of a review and include in the introduction an interpretation of remarks that appear to carry hidden messages.

Changes corresponding to the issues presented in the introduction should be clearly marked in the text unless so much has changed that highlighting or change bars would interfere with readability (assuming sponsor flexibility in this regard). For example, with the reviewers' comments paraphrased in boldface:

Introduction

This is a revised application #JJY654, "Teenage Drinking Patterns," submitted originally on June 1, 1997. We were grateful for the reviewers' thoughtful comments, and their recognition of the significance of our work in terms of "the important impact that such studies will have on early intervention for teenagers at risk for alcoholism." We have made every attempt to respond to the reviewers' concerns as described here. Corresponding changes in the body of the proposal are identified by change bars.

Comments common to the three reviewers:

*1.   **The methods are sketchy and difficult to evaluate.** We have substantially augmented the level of detail in the methods section, including discussion of subject selection, testing, and data analysis (Sections 3.1–3.7, pages 52–59).*

*2.   **There does not appear to be sufficient personnel to carry out the work proposed.** We have revised the budget to include an additional half-time research associate and a full-time postdoctoral fellow (Budget, pages 65–66; Budget justification, page 67).*

Reviewer 1:

*3.   **The discussion of the significance of the work proposed lacks reference to several key papers. It brings into question whether the research team has the background necessary to carry out the proposed work.** In an effort to meet the page limitations of the application, we were deliberately brief in discussing the significance of the proposed work. We certainly regret omitting several key papers, including Jackson, 1993 and Knight,*

1987. In this revised application, we discuss them at greater length. In addition, we would like to emphasize that two members of our research team, Drs. Hird and Allum, did their post-doctoral work with Dr. Jackson, and Dr. Hird maintains a productive collaboration with Dr. Jackson to this date (Section 1, pages 1–2; Budget Justification, page 67).

Reviewer 2:

4.   The investigators should only study teenagers in the age range of 16 to 18 years, since the full range of adolescence represents a corpus of individuals too broad to provide meaningful data.

We respect the reviewer's opinion, but feel that scaling down the study population to represent only the 16- to 18-year age range will unnecessarily limit the research rather than refine it. However, in an effort to be responsive to the reviewer's concern, we have asked Dr. John Greegman, associate professor of statistics, to serve as a consultant to the study. He will be responsible for assisting us with data analysis and interpretation, especially as it pertains to age as a covariant ...

This model would be followed until all concerns of the reviewers are addressed. Should page limitation on the introduction become a problem, favor completeness and brevity over omission of significant issues; minor concerns can be treated summarily at the end.

In general, sponsors that accept revised applications will attempt to have them rereviewed by the original reviewers. Although this affords desirable continuity to the process, it is not a given. There are many examples of revised applications that are reviewed by new reviewers who, whether they agree with the comments of the previous reviewers or not and the manner in which those comments were addressed, will have an entirely new set of concerns that need attention. This is an artifact of a well-intentioned granting process, but a reality. Most sponsors will also limit the number of times that a proposal can be resubmitted; the overall consistency of the comments in successive reviews, therefore, as well as a trend of increasing optimism should be contributing factors in the decision to revise a proposal again or to change direction.

REBUTTALS

Most research funding experts would advise that it is better to prepare a strong resubmission to a proposal that has been declined for
funding, rather than to try to argue against the decision. The philosophy is that reviewers look for quality, not for flaws, and that if a reviewer makes a comment that seems ludicrous, it may be because
the communication of information by the proposer was not clear,
not because the reviewer was inept. Nevertheless, there is no doubt
that some reviews do go awry, and there is no shortage of reasons to
account for them. Yet, despite the unpalatability and frustration of
receiving a review that reads as though it was written about someone else's proposal, formally rebutting the review has at least three
major drawbacks:

1.   Rebuttals are typically conducted in conjunction with the program manager who was responsible for the review and who may ultimately have to serve as an intermediary between a researcher and a
reviewer. A program manager may seek justification for rejection of a
proposal based on overall programmatic grounds, even in the face of
an apparently flawed review, rather than have to moderate a debate
that has the potential to become contentious. Precious time may thus
be wasted in pursuing this avenue.

2.   Once a formal rebuttal is initiated, a proposal cannot, simultaneously, be resubmitted through the traditional channels of the same
sponsor. Pragmatically, this often eliminates the possibility of resubmitting a proposal at the next earliest opportunity and exposing it to
another and hopefully better review.

3.   Even if the rebuttal results in a revised and favorable review, it
is possible that all funds allocated for that review cycle may already
have been distributed. Moreover, there is no guarantee that funds will
be reserved from a subsequent cycle for an appealed proposal. While
discretionary funds may exist in the coffers of sponsors, a successful
rebuttal is not necessarily a direct line to them. Therefore, while the
outcome may be vindicating, it may be extremely costly in time and
effort and still not yield a tangible funding result.

With these cautions in hand, several guidelines can be set forth if a rebuttal is the compelling option:

1. The process should be initiated with a letter to the program manager who handled the review in question. The letter should have three main components:

   • Overall purpose.
   • Specific details about major incorrect statements. Avoid an itemization of minor errors because it can detract from the main arguments about the major deficiencies in the review. However, if minor errors are abundant, a general statement can be made about them.
   • Inquiry as to how to proceed.

For example:

Dear Ms. Kilty,

I am writing to draw to your attention to the review I received of my grant "Teenage Drinking Patterns." In my opinion, the review has significant errors, as outlined here:

1. The reviewer states: **It is unlikely that the PI will reveal anything new about teenage drinking given the significant heterogeneity of her subject groups.** *This is a most unusual comment given the strict inclusion and exclusion criteria described on page 54 of the application, including controls for age, gender, IQ and demographic variables, a power analysis, and the statistical analyses proposed, including an analysis of covariance.*

2. The reviewer also states that: **The PI proposes to use standard neuropsychological tests for group assignment and eventual data analysis, but these tests will provide only weak measures of the patterns she wishes to characterize.** *Although we appreciate the reviewer's careful scrutiny of the neuropsychological batteries we have chosen, unfortunately more sensitive tests do not exist. Moreover, the tests we have chosen are used commonly and with excellent success in studies of*

teenage behavior patterns (please see attached references), in-
cluding a seminal paper published in Science by Phipps et al.,
1996.

In light of these remarks, I feel that my proposal was not re-
viewed with sufficient expertise needed to evaluate its merit. I
wish to request rereview of my proposal, and would appreciate
your guidance as to how to proceed.

Thank you very much.

Sincerely yours,

J. Frint, MD

Director, Adolescent Medicine

2. Throughout all communications with the sponsor, respectfully support the rebuttal with scientific fact on a point-by-point basis; never make derogatory remarks about a reviewer.
3. If the program manager informs you that the case does not warrant further appeal, do not persist. Change your strategy.

SUMMARY

Given the significant effort invested in preparing an outstanding proposal, the months for the review process to take its course often seem to be endless. Nevertheless, it takes time for a sponsor to coordinate the people and the steps in the review process, especially when the scientific review involves a meeting and discussion of proposals by reviewers. With an average waiting time of about 4 to 6 months, and an average funding rate of about 30%, it is important to move forward proactively with more data gathering and project development. When the review finally arrives, and whether or not it is favorable for funding, the feedback should be considered thoughtfully and utilized, as appropriate, to refine research concepts and study designs.

Chapter 10

Interim and Final Reporting

The agreement on the part of the researcher to accept grant funding assumes a commitment to forthrightness about purpose and research goals, to the authenticity of data used to demonstrate proof of concept, and to an ongoing relationship with the sponsor. The commitment to be a research-sponsoring entity requires a commitment to well-articulated priorities and interests, to the assembly of expert reviewers for fair review, to the assurance of sufficient assets to fund grants selected, and to a continuity of the relationship with the researcher after the transfer of funds. The reporting requirements that the researcher must fulfill are the first steps in ensuring that continuity.

When the requirement is for regular interim reporting, the reports secure a lifeline to the sponsor that brings both increasing trust and confidence, as well as ongoing payments on the grant. Singular or final reports serve much the same purpose, but they potentially have the additional goal of creating a tangible link between the ongoing grant and a follow-up proposal for continued support. Although the task of developing reports is usually less taxing than the task of developing the proposals themselves, the requirements for clarity and rigor, coupled with measurable progress, are no less onerous.

Strategies for developing reports and communicating progress and achievements are the focus of this chapter. Chapter 11 is dedicated to the development of competitive funding renewal requests that ideally ensue from a successful funding relationship.

INTERIM REPORTING

Like any other written communication, the sponsor's instructions for reports should be followed precisely. If instructions are not provided, then self-styled reports should be developed in a highly structured way. In either case, the five common scientific sections for reports are:

- Goal and significance of the research.
- Deliverables for the reporting period.
- Results (i.e., progress since funding began if this is the first interim report, or progress since the last reporting period).
- Unexpected results or events for the reporting period.
- Plans for the next reporting period.

These sections are complemented by administrative and budgetary information.

Extensive additional requirements may exist for multicomponent programs, such as the requirement for special codes and descriptions of every project in research centers sponsored by NIH. All requirements should be fulfilled rigorously.

Statement of Overall Goal and Significance

It is important to frame progress in terms of the overall goal and significance of the work being reported. This is consistent with the prevailing philosophy of this book, which is that effective communication is achieved best when ideas are presented within a structured framework and with context. Although this section in a report may often not be more than a paragraph long, it addresses these important criteria by grounding the work. Moreover, since a sponsor may not necessarily look back at an original proposal for reference, this section sets the context for the progress that will be detailed in the subsequent section of the report. For example:

The overall goal of this research is to elucidate and characterize the organic processes underlying the development of insomnia in neurodegenerative disease. Using both waking and sleep electroencephalography (EEG), we will evaluate cortical EEGs and correlate these functional measures with structural mea-

sures of rate and extent of degenerative change obtained by MRI in Alzheimer's, Parkinson's and Pick's Disease. Our goal is to deliver results that will lead directly to the development of effective therapeutic approaches for the alleviation of insomnia in these neurologic diseases.

For this section, it is as acceptable to quote text from the original proposal verbatim as it is to write new text.

Deliverables and Development Goals

This section of the report is dedicated to the deliverables and associated milestones of the project or program. The section should be constructed from a list of deliverables or development goals customized for the reporting period. For example:

The deliverables for this reporting period were:

Technical Goals

(1)   Set-up the EEG monitoring system and finalize procedures for correlating functional and structural measurements.

Clinical Studies

(2)   Recruit and pretest 24 patients with AD, PD, and Pick's Disease (n = 8 per group).

(3)   Conduct data analysis of the 24 patients and identify any pitfalls to the protocol.

(4)   Refine the protocol as necessary and proceed to full-scale testing.

Alternatively, it can be equally effective to provide the complete list of deliverables specified in the original proposal, and highlight in boldface or italics relevant deliverables for the reporting period.

Progress and Results

For each deliverable, progress is defined in terms of where the work is with respect to results, and where the milestones are with respect to the projected timeline. Therefore, space permitting, each relevant result should be itemized and elaborated. This includes, for example, recruitment of personnel, subjects or patients, acquisition and siting of instrumentation, data acquisition, and data analysis.

It is important to discuss only accomplishments in this section. Discussion of obstacles or failures to achieve milestones should be reserved for the subsequent section. The rationale is that, assuming reasonable progress and any reasonable delays, this approach will give the sponsor a chance to fully appreciate the project successes so far. The impact of positive efforts may otherwise become lost in a discussion that at the same time covers tribulations. In fact, even if a project is somewhat astray, it is still advisable to point out the reasonable attempts toward progress in this dedicated section; by using this strategy, even slight progress is justifiably set in counterpart to unexpected occurrences, and in complement to the plan for the coming work period. For example, if subject recruitment has been slow yet consistent or improving, it is far more reassuring to report this activity as:

While we were only able to recruit 10 of the 20 subjects projected for the first year of our study, we experienced a 100% increase in subject recruitment in this second year. With another 100% increase, which we can realistically anticipate given that our new Center is fully operational today, we are confident that we will reach our target 70 subjects by the end of Year 3.

versus

Our subject recruitment has been slower than expected. We have recruited 30 subjects to date (i.e., approximately 40% of the projected target number), leaving 40 subjects to be recruited in the remaining year of the grant.

The lack of clarity about progress, or separation of progress from obstacles, are common downfalls of many reports and can easily jeopardize continued funding. It is important to be positive, clear, and forthright.

To achieve maximum clarity, this section should be subdivided according to deliverables. The section should be further subdivided into appropriate subsections similar to the results section of a manuscript, albeit with lesser or greater detail depending on permitted report length.

Unexpected Occurrences or Results

This section of the report should describe any adverse occurrences during the reporting period, and any results that changed the course of the project outlined in the original experimental plan. Failing a catastrophic event that should be communicated promptly to a sponsor, the following scenarios illustrate some cases.

Scenario 1.   The timeline called for hiring a physical therapist by Month 3 of the project. However, recruitment was more difficult than expected, and resulted in a hire at Month 10. As a consequence, data collection only began at that time.

The discussion may be presented as follows:

Unexpected results or events:

Personnel:

We encountered difficulty in recruiting a physical therapist for this project, despite advertisements in major journals that were placed as soon as we received notice of the grant award. We received six applications in total. We felt that only the sixth applicant—Heria Goppiol, PT, PhD—was the outstanding collaborator we were seeking. Her two-page biographical sketch is attached for your review.

As discussed in Section 2 above, in the short 3 months that Dr. Goppiol has been with the project, she has tested 16 of the 24 patients originally planned for the first 12 months of work. Given the availability of subjects and their high level of compliance with the experimental protocol, we are confident that this delay will be recovered within the next reporting period. Moreover, it does not appear from the data of this first cohort of patients that changes will have to be made to the experimental protocol; the opportunity to proceed with the protocol as originally planned will further accelerate Year 2 progress.

Funds carry-over:

We are requesting carry-over of the unexpended salary support for the 10 months into Year 2 (please see budget).

Scenario 2.   Key instrumentation broke down. It was unavailable for 4 months of the reporting period, during which time 12 subjects were to be tested.

The discussion of this unexpected event may be positively presented as follows:

Unexpected results or events:

We encountered an unfortunate setback in our progress with the failure of our EEG system. The instrumentation was promptly shipped out for repair and returned 4 months later in proper working condition. During this downtime, we focused on the analysis of the data already acquired and obtained encouraging results as described above. Within the first 4 months of Year 2, we fully expect to test subjects scheduled, but not tested, during this period.

Scenario 3.   The first set of experiments yielded negative results, suggesting that one of the alternate approaches considered in the experimental plan as back-up will have to be followed:

Unexpected results or events:

As described above, we successfully recruited 24 patients—8 in each group—to this study. However, we found that sufficient usable data could not be gathered from patients with a fully evolved dementia, and we have revised the experimental plan to exclude these patients. We will augment the number of patients in the other groups to preserve statistical power.

Plans for the Next Reporting Period

This section should summarize the deliverables for the next reporting period succinctly, ideally in the context of the accomplishments reported in the present one. This will ensure that continuity and logical progression are key factors in the evolution of the work. For example:

> *Given the success we have had in reaching our project goals for the first reporting period, including patient recruitment and completion of the first series of test, our goals for the next period are unchanged from the original experimental plan. By the end of the next reporting period—Year 2 of this 3-year project—we hope to have completed 80% of the patient testing and have sufficient data to present at the upcoming 1999 meeting of the Society for Neurosciences. The remaining 20% of the data collection will be completed during the first quarter of Year 3. Extensive data analysis and manuscript preparation will take place during the last three quarters of the project period.*

FINAL REPORTS

Although the structure of final reports is not unlike interim reports, the emphasis is different. Here, the report is focused on the progress and results of the entire project, rather than on the accomplishments of component reporting periods. Therefore, the final report should be laid out in a framework that provides the overall goal, the project or program deliverables, details of the experimental work carried out, results, and conclusions.

Emphasis on hurdles that may have been encountered during the funding period should be limited because details of delays or obstacles that were significant for interim reporting may be less significant by the time the entire project is completed. For example, although recruitment of personnel or instrument breakage may have been a major obstacle in a given reporting period, they are essentially irrelevant if the project was ultimately completed as planned. Therefore, such details may be omitted in the final report unless they either truly impacted the final direction of the project or would impact the direction that future related work will take.

Sponsors' requirements for final reports vary, with certain sponsors requiring that a final report be submitted as an independent self-standing document, and some requiring that the final report is submitted as an independent document as well as part of the prior work section or an appendix of a new proposal. Regardless of how the final report is filed, however, or how many times it is filed, the two most critical sections of the final report are the results and conclusions. As always, the results must be presented in a structured and rigorous way. The conclusion must then draw on the results to demonstrate project success, and to highlight the next projects that need to be undertaken in pursuit of the overall program goal. This serves as the crucial link, therefore, to any future related proposal that may be made to the same sponsor.

SUMMARY

Interim reports serve to assure a sponsor that stepwise progress toward deliverables is being achieved in a manner that is logical and timely. Interim reports are also used as examples of the quality of the sponsor's or program manager's portfolio to *their* sponsors (e.g., Congress in the United States). Interim reports must demonstrate, therefore, both scientific progress and compliance with the terms of the project award. The final report is the final chapter in the life of a grant and, ideally, is the set-up for the upcoming one. Therefore, final reports must deliver final results of projects, situate the new results in the context of the overall research program, and successfully lead a sponsor to welcome a request for continued funding.

Chapter 11

Competing Renewals

Competing renewals are developed to continue project-based and multicomponent research for a cycle of funding that closely follows the existing one. Because these renewals request support beyond the original funding period, they are evaluated competitively against other proposals. Some sponsors, such as a subset of those funding SBIRs and STTRs, only permit competing renewals after the full completion of the first period of work; others accept proposals for competing renewals at any review cycle during an existing funding period provided that they pass the test of reasonableness with respect to timing. The considerations and trade-offs are:

- Time remaining on the original grant.
- Number of milestones completed and quality of the results.
- Time needed for review of the new proposal (including processing time and potentially resubmission time).
- Desirability of avoiding a lapse in funding.

Many sponsors are preferentially predisposed to funding researchers with whom they already have a relationship, especially if the research has culminated in significant contributions to a field. It is clearly a natural tendency for a sponsor to invest in a researcher with demonstrated success, especially if that success can be at least partly attributed to the support of that sponsor. To some extent, knowing which sponsors are likely to favor a continued relationship may be useful in the strategic development of a research funding plan, but there are no hard rules or lists to provide as guidelines. Therefore, the decision about whether to pursue continued funding resides foremost in the first critical node in the final conceptualization pathways described here and illustrated in Fig. 11.1 and Fig. 11.2.

CONCEPTUALIZING COMPETING RENEWALS OF PROJECT-BASED RESEARCH

The Quality and Nature of Results of the Existing Funding Period Justify Continued Funding

The first decision in this pathway (Fig.11.1) queries the overall quality and nature of results from the existing funding period. It embodies the decisions in the original project-based pathway regarding program fit, match with a sponsor, and merit. Assuming that it is appropriate to submit a competing continuation from the point of view of the project timeline (e.g., the project is at least in the third year of a 4- or 5-year project), at this first point in the pathway, there are three possibilities:

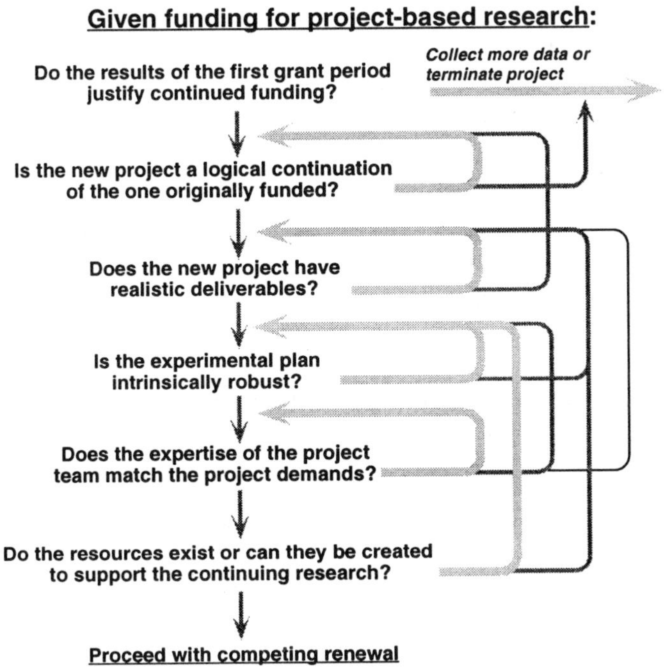

FIG. 11.1. Conceptualization pathway for competing renewal of project-based research.

1. The quality of the research is high and the nature of the findings naturally leads to the need for more research.
2. The quality of the research is high but the nature of the findings marks the end of that successful research direction.
3. The quality of the research is low, and the nature of the findings do not suggest that continued investment in that research direction is merited.

The first possibility is the one that justifies progress along the conceptualization pathway and the proposal for continued funding. Further considerations about timing the proposal submission are then affected by subsequent decisions lower in the pathway.

The second possibility is a laudable overall outcome, but will not lead to a competitive proposal. The third possibility will also not lead to a competitive proposal, but with a less satisfactory outcome unless more research is carried out to reverse the prevailing assessment. Both lead to a new direction.

The New Project is a Logical Continuation of the One Originally Funded

Continuity of overall research direction from one project period to the next is necessary for continued funding success. As discussed in chapters 1 and 2, there is considerable room to extend and expand ideas, but a fit should not be forced. If the fit appears to be contrived, then the new concept should either be revised, or the existence of the second possibility recognized and a new direction pursued.

Deliverables, Methods, Project Team Expertise, Resources

The following four decisions are the same as the analogous decisions in the pathway for first-time, project-based research (chapter 2). They are:

- The continuing research has realistic deliverables.
- The experimental plan for the continuing research is intrinsically robust.
- The expertise of the project team matches the demands of the continuing research.

- The resources exist or can be created to support the continuing research.

As before, the criteria for each decision should be met before proceeding to the next one.

CONCEPTUALIZING COMPETING RENEWALS OF MULTICOMPONENT RESEARCH PROGRAMS

The Program Accomplishments of the First Funding Period Should Justify Continued Funding

This first decision in this pathway (Fig. 11.2) queries the overall success of a multicomponent program and the contributions it has made.

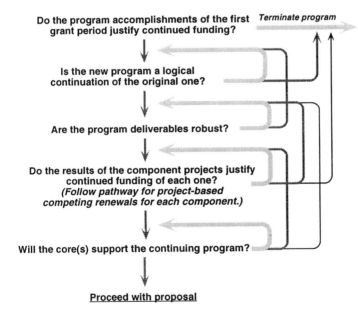

FIG. 11.2. Conceptualization pathway for competing renewal of multicomponent research programs.

It queries whether the program, as a whole, has been the host to important scientific results, valuable collaborations and, as appropriate, successful students, and educational and informational programs. The evaluation of the criteria for this decision is complex and multifaceted, therefore, and relies intimately on the deliverables originally outlined.

The New Program Should Be a Logical Continuation of the Original One

Multicomponent programs, by definition, have many personalities. It is the composite of the characteristics of the new program that should be naturally consistent with the characteristics of the previous one, and the new program should be developed with familiar philosophy and continuous overall goals. Depending on the outcome of the evaluation of the individual program subcomponents—an analysis conducted lower down in the pathway—meeting the criterion of logical continuity will fall somewhere on a scale of obvious to extremely tenuous. The position on the scale will be determined by the number of new project subcomponents that replace existing ones. Tenuous continuity due to too great a programmatic shift will compromise competitiveness. Iterations at this point are important, therefore, to create an optimum balance between continuing and prospective new subcomponents.

The Program Deliverables Are Robust

Consistent with previous discussions, the deliverables for a continuing program should be well-defined and realistic with respect to time and budget.

The Results of Each Subcomponent Project Justify Continued Funding of That Project

This node specifically considers the quality and nature of the research of each subcomponent project. Here, therefore, the pathway for conceptualizing project-based continuations should be followed for each compnent. Any project that should not be continued can be replaced by another, provided that the number of entirely new projects replacing existing ones does not compromise the requirement for logical continuity.

The Core(s) Support
the Continuing Program

It is not a given that the core components of an existing program are perfectly suited to the new one. Each core should be specifically revisited, therefore, and accepted, eliminated, or augmented as needed.

SUMMARY

It is enviable to be in the position in which successful research efforts justify renewed funding. With the exception of the first two decisions in the two conceptualization pathways presented in this chapter, the approach to developing a request for continued funding mimics that of the earlier pathways. The task should be familiar, therefore, although not necessarily less daunting.

The format for competing renewals will also be familiar, with two distinctions: (a) the sponsor's instructions for applications may have changed since the last submission, and (b) the new application contains the final report, in part or in full as described previously, for the existing grant.

Attention to the details about the sponsor's needs—even a sponsor with whom a relationship exists—and attention to scientific and administrative detail in the proposing document are determining factors for continued funding success.

Chapter 12

Concluding Remarks

The requirement for sponsored research funding is sometimes viewed as a relentless evil that distracts the serious researcher from the laboratory and science. This can indeed be the case when the process is approached in a haphazard and unstructured way. The other and far more desirable way to look at research funding is that it is a component of daily research life that is creative and empowering. The creative, successful search for funds is led by thinking and planning, where the thinking defines the direction of the research, and the planning secures the right mechanisms and right sponsors for it. The strategic preparation culminates in a proposal that ideally delivers to a prospective sponsor the expression of a genuine match in interest and priority, and an end-product of high scientific integrity. On the one hand, the process may be arduous and unforgiving, but on the other, substantial funds exist nationally and internationally for persistent and deserving researchers and for meritorious research.

Research funding brings to the researcher more than just the opportunity to carry out experiments—it brings fiscal and professional autonomy. It also brings mutually beneficial and potentially long-lasting relationships with sponsors, and it brings enduring contributions to society. The final message of this book, therefore, is one of encouragement—encouragement to be inspired by scientific advancement, accepting of peer review, gracious in peer review service, and to utilize research success well beyond the walls of the laboratory to influence science and science policy worldwide.

References

Bergan, H. (1996). *Where the information is: A guide to electronic research for nonprofit organizations.* Virginia: Bioguide Press.

Herring, K. L. (Ed.). (1994). *American Psychological Association's guide to research support.* Washington, DC: American Psychological Association.

Rich, E. H. (Ed.). (1996). *Guide to funding for international and foreign programs.* New York: The Foundation Center.

Index

V

Vaccines, 66
Visiting scholars, 57

W

Whitaker Foundation, 6